Ayn

Rand

and

Business

Ayn
Rand
and
Business

DONNA
GREINER

&

THEODORE B.
KINNI

TEXERE

Published by

TEXERE
55 East 52nd Street
New York, NY 10055

Tel: +1 (212) 317 5106
Fax: +1 (212) 317 5178
www.etexere.com

In the UK:

TEXERE Publishing Limited
71-77 Leadenhall Street
London EC3A 3DE
www.etexere.co.uk

Tel: +44 (0)20 7204 3644
Fax: +44 (0)20 7208 6701

This publication is designed to provide accurate and authoritative information in regard to the subject matter covered. It is sold with the understanding that the publisher is not engaged in rendering legal, accounting, or other professional services. If legal advice or other expert assistance is required, the services or a competent professional person should be sought.

Book design by Victoria Kuskowski

Library of Congress Cataloging-in-Publication Data is available.

ISBN 1-58799-072-5

Printed in the United States of America.

This book is printed on acid-free paper

10 9 8 7 6 5 4 3 2 1

Contents

CONTENTS

3
RANDIAN MANAGEMENT

Introduction

Most businesspeople don't think of themselves as heroic characters and, by and large, our culture does not support such an image. From the negative appellation "robber barons," applied to the business giants of the nineteenth century, to Sinclair Lewis's novel *Babbit* (1922) to Oliver Stone's film *Wall Street* (1987), commerce regularly plays the villain in our society. It is a portrayal that Ayn Rand passionately and unceasingly fought throughout her life.

Rand cherished and celebrated business, especially the heavy industries that dominated American business during her lifetime and the entrepreneurs who founded and built them. Rand called them "the motor of the world" and the "prime movers" of society. She wrote two best-selling novels, *The Fountainhead* and *Atlas Shrugged*, and constructed a philosophy known as Objectivism to prove that her epic image of business was the right one. Along the way, in an astonishing journey, she transformed herself from a shopkeeper's daughter in St. Petersburg, Russia, to one of the world's leading advocates of laissez-faire capitalism. *Ayn Rand and Business* begins with that story.

Born in 1905, Rand reached the pinnacle of her career during the 1960s. Her best-selling novel of ideas, *Atlas*

Shrugged, had been published in 1957, and even though it received little critical acclaim, the book's sales grew steadily stronger as readers recommended it to one another. By 1963, 1.2 million copies of the book had been sold and many of its fans were clamoring to learn more about the Objectivist philosophy on which it is based. Ayn Rand clubs were established around the country, and live and taped lecture series were consistently oversubscribed.

During the period between the release of *Atlas Shrugged* and the early 1970s, Rand gave up novels and wrote nonfiction almost exclusively. Along with a handful of her most loyal followers, she spent her time explaining the tenets of Objectivism and applying them to real world examples. In a pitched battle of ideas, she set out to prove that objective reality, reason, self-interest, and capitalism provided the essential elements of an integrated philosophy for living. Although it would be an exaggeration to say she converted the world, she did exert a significant influence on those who came into contact with her ideas. Federal Reserve Chairman Alan Greenspan was a member of Rand's inner circle for fifteen years, the Libertarian Party is based in part on Objectivism, and business gurus, such as George Gilder, have used it as a basis for their own thinking. *Ayn Rand and Business* explores the primary elements and the promise of Objectivism.

The late 1960s proved to be the climatic peak in Rand's life. In the 1970s, she suffered lung cancer, depression, and the mental decline and death of her husband of fifty years,

Frank O'Connor. In the early 1980s, she became increasingly reclusive and, in 1982, she died of cardiopulmonary failure. Still, Rand's thinking continues to reverberate through our world.

Two decades after her death, her ideas are studied among academic philosophers and she is a popular figure in contemporary culture. More than 20 million copies of Rand's books have been sold since 1936, according to a news release from the Ayn Rand Institute. Her books currently sell more than 400,000 copies each year. In 1995, *Newsweek* surveyed the media interest in her life and books and concluded, "she's everywhere."[1] In 1997 and 1998, two feature films based on her life were released; one of them, the documentary *Ayn Rand: A Sense of Life*, was nominated for an Academy Award. In 1999, the United States Post Office honored Rand with a commemorative stamp, an especially odd tribute for that institution to make to a woman who fiercely argued for the privatization of all governmental activities not directly related to the protection of individual rights. But it was just a minor irony in a story filled with ironies.

In fact, as you will see, irony is a consistent theme in Ayn Rand's life. The greatest irony is that Rand's philosophy, which is based on individual rights, somehow resulted in a cultlike organization that obeyed her without hesitation and excommunicated members who dared to question her edicts. To this day, there is an ongoing firefight between warring Objectivist factions.

Unfortunately, the controversies that swirl around Rand can obscure the practical nature of her legacy and intimidate those who would like to learn more. Three generations of people have read and applauded *The Fountainhead* and *Atlas Shrugged*, but out of the millions who were inspired by their first exposure to Rand's ideas, comparatively few have pushed beyond the novels to understand the basic elements of Objectivism and incorporate her ideas into their lives. That is especially unfortunate because much of Rand's philosophical thinking can be applied with great success to career and management. *Ayn Rand and Business* focuses on the practical benefits of Objectivism.

To Rand, philosophy—the study of the laws and causes of reality—provides the foundational beliefs by which you live your life. If you refuse to consider carefully and live by your own beliefs, you will, by default, be forced to live by someone else's. What holds true for life also holds true for career. Either you will work and manage according to your own dictates or you will be at the mercy of someone else's.

Ayn Rand was intensely focused on, and perhaps finally consumed by, the quest to learn how people can reach their full potential. To her, that potential meant productive work, that is, the creation of goods and services and the profits that result from those activities.

Rand was also driven to teach to others what she had produced by the power of her own mind. The philosophy of Objectivism was intended to be the ultimate success formula.

Rand wanted to show people how to achieve their individual dreams and, in doing so, effortlessly contribute to the well being of everyone else.

Objectivism requires a strict adherence to reality. Whether people choose to recognize it or not, existence exists, said Rand, and they are capable of knowing that reality. Objectivism demands that we use our brains. Rand identified reason as mankind's only source of knowledge and survival. Objectivism identifies a morality — a code of behavioral virtues — that supports reason, purpose, and self-esteem. Rand understood that a philosophy that could not be acted upon was useless. Put into business terms, Objectivism yields independent, thinking people who follow a consistent, productive set of values in pursuit of knowable markets. These are the fundamental elements of a successful business and work life.

Which brings us to an overview of the content of this book. In late 1940s, an Associated Press reporter interviewed Rand as she was preparing the screenplay for the film version of *The Fountainhead*. They talked about her next novel and Rand told the reporter, "[I]t will combine metaphysics, morality, economics, politics, and sex..."[2] Now, we aren't suggesting that this book rivals, or even vaguely approaches, the accomplishment of *Atlas Shrugged*, but the elements that Rand listed during her interview are the same elements that permeated her life and thought. To that extent, they are also a good description of the contents of this book.

Ayn Rand and Business explores Rand's life and describes

her ideas from a layman's perspective. The book examines the implications and applications of Rand's thinking for the business reader. It shows how Randian ideas and concepts can be applied in a business career and in the management of organizations. Here is an advance look at the three-part presentation that lies ahead:

The opening section of the book consists of three chapters designed to introduce Ayn Rand and Objectivism. They set the stage for understanding Rand's applications to career and management by providing an understanding of her life and the development of her philosophy. The first two chapters tell Ayn Rand's life story from her birth in Russia in 1905 to her death in 1982. Like Rand's legacy, the story continues to the present day and explores the evolution of the Objectivist philosophical movement since her death. The third chapter provides an overview of Objectivism. It explains the principle assumptions and tenets of Objectivism and shows how they combine to create a worldview, or what Rand described as an integrated philosophy for living.

The second section of the book, *Randian Work*, contains eight chapters that hone in on Rand's ideas regarding the personal characteristics of effective people. The ethical system that Rand created offers clear guidelines for the actions and behavior of people. The first chapter in part two sets out the values, or goals, that people must strive for in order to become successful. Rand defined these values as reason, purpose, and self-esteem. Part two's chapters also explore the seven virtues, or behaviors, that allow people to achieve the Randian values. The book devotes a chapter to each of them: rationality, which corresponds to the Randian value of reason; productiveness, which corresponds to purpose; and pride, which corresponds to self-esteem. Four additional chapters cover rationality's supporting virtues: independence, integrity, honesty, and justice. The values and virtues of Objectivism are at their best when applied to a business career. Before you can successfully manage and lead others, you must first learn to think and act effectively on your own.

Part three of the book, *Randian Management,* takes the next step shifting perspective from the individual businessperson to managing business organizations. Its three chapters explore Rand's ideas for managing and leading organizations. They cover topics such as entrepreneurship and innovation, people management, vision, and long-term thinking. For further study, we've included a bibliography of Rand's books and an annotated selection of books about her by other authors.

By the end of this book, you will know why Ayn Rand is important in today's world and why she will continue to be influential in the future.

Ayn Rand taught people how to become producers and traders and urged them to earn a spot among the world's prime movers. If you take the time to understand and act on her ideas, perhaps you too will fulfill that goal. In that case, you will certainly understand why Ayn Rand matters.

1

Ayn

Rand

and

Objectivism

1

THE JOURNEY TO FREEDOM AND PROSPERITY

ON SEPTEMBER 4, 1926, a stunned twenty-one-year-old Russian girl stepped into Cecil B. DeMille's roadster. "I was so breathlessly numb that to this day I can remember the feeling," she explained three decades later.[1] Her emotions were only natural; the girl was stepping into her dreams. She had already escaped the fate of the dispossessed bourgeoisie of Soviet Russia and had begun her transformation into a screenwriter named Ayn Rand. And now, within hours of arriving in Hollywood, one in a multitude of unknown and unexpected young people, she was being driven to the set of the epic movie *The King of Kings* by one of the film industry's most powerful men.

On that day, Ayn Rand completed the first stage and the

most unlikely leg of her own epic. It was a rebirth that had started nine months earlier when she left Leningrad for the last time.

Alisa Rosenbaum in Russia

St. Petersburg is where Ayn Rand was born Alisa Zinovievna Rosenbaum on February 2, 1905.[2] Alisa was the first of three daughters born to Zinovy Zacharovich and his wife, Anna Borisovna. Zinovy was a successful chemist who owned his own pharmacy. He was a quiet, serious man who took pride in his accomplishments and his rise out of the poverty of his youth. Anna was the more socially inclined of the pair. She enjoyed the arts and hosting parties.

The Rosenbaums were Jewish, but religion did not play a significant role in their lives. The family was prosperous and able to afford two-month summer vacations on the Black Sea. In the summer of 1914, when Alisa was nine years old, they enjoyed an extended vacation to Austria and Switzerland, which ended abruptly with the outbreak of World War I.

Alisa, by her own account, was not comfortable in casual social situations. She was largely friendless and, rather than adjust her somewhat intense personality, preferred to spend her time alone. The young girl's saving grace was her intelligence. She was precocious and taught herself to read and write, gaining early acceptance into school. School, however, proved to be something less than a worthy challenge.

"I went to different schools in two different cities and I was the top student in them," said Ayn Rand decades later. "I always tried to sit in the back row of the class and I put a book in front of me and I was writing novels from the age of ten. I was writing screenplays at eight, but I was writing novels in class, otherwise I would be terribly bored."[3]

In February 1917, the Russian Revolution demolished Alisa's world. Czar Nicholas II abdicated his throne and the Duma, the existing parliament, took control of Russia and its capital, Petrograd, formerly St. Petersberg. In October, the Duma was forcibly removed when the Bolsheviks, led by Vladimir Lenin, stormed the city's Winter Palace, capturing political control and instituting a communist system. Shortly thereafter, the city's businesses and banks were nationalized. The Rosenbaum pharmacy was seized by the Red Army; it was now the property of the people, and thus, at age twelve, Alisa's life-long opposition to communism was established.

In late 1918, with the Russian civil war raging, Red-occupied Petrograd collapsing into chaos, and no prospects for improvement, the Rosenbaum family left their home on a dangerous journey to reach the Crimea, which was under the control of the White Army. On their arrival in Odessa, Alisa's father opened a small shop and began rebuilding their lives. But they soon found themselves in the middle of a seesaw battle between the Red and White Armies for control of the Crimea.

In 1921, the Red Army won the war, and Russia. Alisa, by this time a high school graduate, was contributing to the family income by teaching Red soldiers to read and write. The sixteen-year-old was now fully committed to systematic and logical thinking, and the foundations for her beliefs were established. Alisa had declared her atheism, rejecting religion because no proof of God's existence could be offered, and championed individualism, rejecting the collective nature of communism as evil.

Refusing to flee Russia altogether, Zinovy Rosenbaum decided to return to Petrograd with his family. They arrived home to find food shortages and political repression. They lived in the same building they had left, but in a much smaller apartment with no water or electricity. In one area, however, the communist regime had worked in Alisa's favor. Tuition had been abolished at the University of Petrograd and the degree programs had been shortened from five to three years. On October 2, 1921, she enrolled in the university after deciding on a major in history and a minor in philosophy.

Alisa's college years coincided with a running ideological battle over the content taught at the University. "I went to a Soviet university," she explained in 1974. "At that time there were still some good professors who were actually teaching subjects, but there was also a great deal of propaganda and it did not affect me in the least."[4]

By the end of her schooling, however, the Marxists were firmly in control. By 1924, students from bourgeoisie families were being expelled and those who dared to criticize communism were arrested and sent to labor camps in Siberia. Alisa eluded the student purge because of her impending graduation and she received her degree on July 15 that year.[5]

Alisa's mother arranged a part-time job for the nineteen-year-old graduate as a tour guide at Peter and Paul Fortress, where she lectured on the site's history. In the fall of 1924, she returned to school. This time, she enrolled in Leningrad's (Petrograd was renamed once again after Lenin's death) All-Union State Institute of Cinematography to learn screenwriting.

By early 1925, inspired partly by the views of New York City she saw in movies, Alisa became convinced that she should leave Russia. Relatives of Anna Rosenbaum lived in Chicago and Anna asked them if Alisa could visit. They agreed. In the fall of the year, Alisa was granted a passport for a six-month journey and, in January 1926, she left Leningrad with three hundred dollars and a first-class passage to America for which Anna had sold her jewelry. Alisa also took her Remington-Rand typewriter.

There seems to have been little question in Alisa's mind that the visit would be permanent. "I would no more have thought of returning than of jumping off a building," she later declared.[6]

THE TRANSFORMATION INTO AYN RAND

In February 1926, shortly after her twenty-first birthday, Alisa landed in New York. A few days later, she arrived in Chicago and moved in with the extended family of her mother's uncle, Harry Portnoy. Alisa seems to have been something of a mystery to her Midwestern relatives, but she had a plan for her future. The young Russian devoted all of her time to learning English, going to the cinema owned by her family, and writing screen scenarios for the then-silent movies.

By the time her visa expired, Alisa had completed four screenplays, each translated into English by a cousin. The Portnoy clan arranged to extend her visa and gave Alisa one hundred dollars, a train ticket to Los Angeles, and a letter of introduction to the publicity department at the DeMille Studios. So, in September 1926, when Alisa Rosenbaum should have been back home in Leningrad, Ayn Rand was arriving in Hollywood. The new last name came from her typewriter; the first name, Ayn ("rhymes with mine," wrote Alvin Toffler in Rand's 1964 interview for Playboy magazine), was a twist on the Finnish name Aina.[7]

On her first day in Los Angeles, Ayn secured lodgings at the Hollywood Studio Club, an inexpensive residential hotel for single women trying to break into the film industry. Over the years, the Studio Club, which operated under the auspices of the YWCA and was supported by the film industry, offered a secure home base for other notables such as Marilyn Monroe, Donna Reed, and Kim Novak.

On her second day on the West Coast, after a fruitless interview at the DeMille Studios, Ayn was leaving the grounds when she found herself staring in awe at the studio head himself. Perhaps it was her piercing eyes that caused Cecil B. DeMille to ask what she was doing there and, when Ayn explained her goal of becoming a screenwriter, to invite her to spend the day on the set of his latest movie. For a week, DeMille gave Ayn a daily pass to watch the making of *The King of Kings*, and then he gave her a job as an extra. The job paid $7.50 per day and lasted several months. It also provided the setting for the first meeting between Ayn and Frank O'Connor, a bit player on that movie who was trying to establish his own film career.

DeMille arranged to have Ayn's screenplays read, but they were not deemed worthy of production. Nevertheless, when the shooting of *The King of Kings* was completed, he did hire her as junior screenwriter. Ayn read and summarized the studio's literary properties and suggested how they might be adapted to film. She worked for DeMille until he closed his studio in 1928.

The completion of *The King of Kings* also caused Ayn great pain. She had fallen in love with Frank O'Connor, but it was an unspoken love, and when the movie ended she lost her sole contact point with the handsome actor. Months later, by chance, Ayn met Frank once again and, this time, they began a formal relationship.

After the DeMille Studios closed, Ayn struggled to support herself by working a variety of temporary, low-paying jobs. She remained committed to a writing career, completing film synopses and short stories and planning a novel, which was never written. "From now on—no thought whatever about yourself, only about your work," she instructed herself in one of her journals. "You don't exist. You are only a writing engine. Don't stop, until you really and *honestly* know that you *cannot* go on."[8]

One month before her final visa extension was set to expire, on April 15, 1929, Ayn married Frank and gained both a husband and legal residence in the United States. In 1931, she became a naturalized citizen. Soon after, she also found steady work in the wardrobe department of RKO Pictures. She disliked the job, but it and the small acting assignments her contacts at RKO offered to Frank helped the newly married couple to weather the start of the Great Depression in good form.

Ayn put her financial stability to good use and continued to write throughout this period. She started work on another novel that would become *We the Living*, but found her still-inadequate command of written English made it difficult to properly express herself. So she stopped work and wrote two screenplays. In 1932, Universal Pictures bought one of them, *Red Pawn*, for fifteen hundred dollars, an amount equivalent to more than two years of her RKO salary. Ayn's first response was to resign her position. Six years after leaving Russia, Ayn Rand had achieved her dream of becoming a professional screenwriter.

A MAJOR NOVELIST EMERGES

Red Pawn, the story of a Russian woman who becomes the lover of the commandant of a Communist political prison in order to save the life of her husband who is incarcerated there, never made it onto the silver screen.[9] Nevertheless, it established Ayn's career. She went back to work on *We the Living* with renewed vigor for almost a year until early 1933, when money again became an issue and she decided to earn more by writing a play.

Penthouse Legend was completed that same year. The play was inspired by the true story of Ivar Kreuger, the so-called Match King who committed suicide in 1932 after the collapse of his worldwide business empire, dedicated to the production and sale of matches. It contained what Ayn called a "gimmick," her idea to create a play around a trial that would choose the jury from the audience. MGM bought an option to turn the play into a movie, but once again, it was not filmed and Ayn went back to work on *We the Living*.

By end of 1933, Ayn finished *We the Living*, her first novel. Similarly to *Red Pawn*, the story featured a Russian woman who takes a Communist lover to save her true love, an anti-Communist who needs food and medicine in order to survive. The setting, 1920s Petrograd, drew directly on the author's life experience. The story illustrated her view of the nature of collectivist ideologies.

"*We the Living* is not a story about Soviet Russia in 1925," Ayn wrote in her introduction to the 1959 revised edition of the novel. "It is a story about Dictatorship, any dictatorship, anywhere, at any time… What the rule of brute force does to men and how it destroys the best…"[10] She was unable to find a publisher for the book for two years.

Ayn had better luck, financially if not esthetically, with *Penthouse Legend.* It was first brought to the stage as *Woman on Trial* for a short run in Hollywood in 1934, and in September 1935 a production mounted by A.H. Woods opened on Broadway. Ayn and Frank moved to New York to help stage the play, which was renamed *Night of January 16th.* Working with Woods was a bitter experience for Ayn, who found herself fighting to retain the work's most important ideas. "The rest of the play's history was hell," she wrote in the introduction to the 1968 edition. "The entire period before and after the play's opening was a sickening struggle between Woods and me."[11]

The play, however, was a success with audiences and, perhaps because of its popularity, The Macmillan Company purchased *We the Living* and paid Ayn a $250 advance on royalties for her four years of work. *Night of January 16th* ran for six months and paid the writer as much as twelve hundred dollars per week. Ayn's newfound prosperity enabled her to begin the difficult, and ultimately unsuccessful, process of bringing her parents and two sisters to the United States. After more than two years' efforts, on May 31, 1937, she received the final word from Leningrad. The telegram read simply, "CANNOT GET PERMISSION."

We the Living was published in March 1936 and received little immediate attention from either the critics or the public. It took a year for word-of-mouth sales to begin to build, but by then, Macmillan had destroyed the type for the book and would not reset it after the initial printing of three thousand copies was sold. (Ayn's first novel would remain out-of-print in the United States until 1959.)

Starting in 1935, Ayn began planning a new novel with the working title *Second-Hand Lives.* "The first purpose of the book is *a defense of egoism in its real meaning,* egoism as a new faith," she wrote in a journal entry dated December 4, 1935.[12] Ayn spent a good deal of time on research for the new novel, even working in an architectural firm in a clerical position. She did not actually start writing the book that would be published as *The Fountainhead* until June 1938.

In between, Ayn wrote *Anthem,* a short novel set in a future in which the word "I" does not exist. Cassell, the English house that had published *We the Living,* released *Anthem* in 1938, but no American publisher could be found for the book until 1945. Meanwhile, Ayn adapted *We the Living* for the stage in 1939. It opened on February 14, 1940, as *The Un-conquered* and closed to negative reviews in five days.

Even though money was again becoming an issue, Ayn and Frank volunteered to work on behalf of Wendell Willkie in 1940's presidential election. Again, she was disappointed. As the campaign progressed, Willkie began compromising his platform and on Election Day, Franklin Roosevelt won by a landslide. Ayn never agreed with liberal politics and now became disillusioned with the conservatives as well. Not wanting to be aligned with either, she began to define herself as a "radical for capitalism."

Down to a few hundred dollars in savings, Ayn tried to use the opening chapters of *The Fountainhead* to land a publishing contract for the book. It was rejected by twelve publishers. No one believed a philosophical novel had any commercial appeal. With savings running out, Ayn was forced to take work as a reader for Paramount Pictures. The six to ten dollars that she received for synopses helped her survive until finally, in December 1941, Bobbs-Merrill agreed to publish *The Fountainhead* and offered Ayn a $1,000 advance. She wrote the final two-thirds of the book in one year, delivering the completed manuscript on December 31, 1942.

In May 1943, *The Fountainhead* debuted to less than stellar sales. The now-famous novel of individualism received almost uniformly negative reviews. But those readers who did discover it loved the controversial sex scene between

Howard Roark and Dominique Francon, Roark's climatic destruction of the public housing complex, and, for some deeper thinkers, the rational egoism that provided the philosophic foundation for the book and Ayn's conception of the ideal man. And they told other readers. By late 1943, the book's sales had reached 18,000, and then Hollywood came calling. Ayn demanded and got $50,000 for movie rights from Warner Brothers.

Ayn and Frank returned to Los Angeles, so Ayn could write the preliminary script for the movie. They bought a contemporary house designed by Richard Neutra, a student of Frank Lloyd Wright, on thirteen acres in Chatsworth and a Cadillac convertible. The movie version of *The Fountainhead*, starring Gary Cooper and Patricia Neal, did not appear until six years later in 1949, but the book's sales continued to grow throughout the 1940s. Even two decades after its author's death, it still sells more than 100,000 copies per year. Ayn Rand's financial struggles were over forever.

2

THE
LEADER
OF
OBJECTIVISM

BY 1950, AYN RAND was writing a new book that she had begun planning five years earlier. Its working title was *The Strike*, and the forty-five-year-old author intended it to be the ultimate statement of her philosophy. The book's plot had grown from a question she had asked during a phone conversation with a friend in 1943: "What would happen if *all* the creative minds of the world went on strike?"[1] *The Strike*, which was published as *Atlas Shrugged*, would be the answer.

A CULT IS BORN

Ayn had attracted a solid base of fans by 1950, and one of them in particular would have an enormous impact on her life. After exchanging several letters in late 1949 and early

1950, Ayn invited Nathan Blumenthal, a nineteen-year-old psychology student at UCLA, to visit her and Frank at their home to discuss philosophy. Nathan arrived on the evening of March 2, 1950, and they talked through the night.

Later, Ayn told him, "Walking into the living room, seeing you for the first time, I thought, He's got my kind of face. And then I told myself, Don't start that again, meaning, Don't start hoping. I'd met too many alleged admirers who seemed intelligent and serious in their values and who turned out to be phonies. But, you see, this time it didn't end in disappointment. This time I was right."[2]

The young Canadian, along with his girlfriend, Barbara Weidman, was soon visiting Ayn and Frank on a regular basis, and a close personal relationship developed. Ayn read the pair the completed portions of *Atlas Shrugged* and discussed her philosophical beliefs. The young couple introduced Ayn to their relatives and friends, including Leonard Peikoff, Barbara's seventeen-year-old cousin, who after meeting Ayn was inspired to abandon his plans to study medicine and take up philosophy.

In the summer of 1951, Barbara and Nathan left California to continue their schooling in New York City. Soon after, Ayn decided she could no longer work in California. In October, with the new novel almost two-thirds complete, she and Frank also relocated to New York. It was to remain their home for the rest of their lives.

During the early 1950s, Nathan and Barbara were instrumental in the creation of a sort of salon that revolved around Ayn and met in her apartment on Saturday evenings. Ayn called the group the "Class of '43" after the publication date of *The Fountainhead*; they jokingly referred to themselves as the "Collective." The group was composed of friends and relatives of Nathan and Barbara, including Leonard Peikoff, who had also moved to New York, and Alan Greenspan, now chairman of the Federal Reserve. All of them were decades younger than Ayn.

The reunion in New York also intensified the social relationship between Ayn and Frank and Nathan and Barbara. They often spent four and five evenings each week together. Ayn encouraged her young friends to marry, and, in January 1953, she and Frank served as the matron of honor and best man at their wedding. In the fall of 1954, Nathan followed Ayn's example and legally changed his name to Nathaniel Branden.

Shortly thereafter, Ayn and Nathaniel shocked their respective spouses by declaring their love for each other and asking for permission to meet alone one afternoon and one evening each week. These meetings were supposed to be nonsexual, but soon after the meetings began, Ayn and Nathaniel wanted to begin a full-blown love affair. After weeks of cajoling, Frank and Barbara gave their consent.

The reluctant agreement took its toll. For the next two years, Ayn and Nathaniel kept regularly scheduled trysts. Frank would often pass Nathaniel at the apartment door, leaving so his wife and her lover could enjoy their privacy. Frank spent the ensuing hours at a local bar and began drinking heavily. Barbara began suffering anxiety attacks.[3]

Ayn, meanwhile, was buried in the creation of the most complete statement of her philosophy to date, the sixty-page radio speech that John Galt broadcasts near the end of *Atlas Shrugged*. Ayn spent two years, between 1953 and 1955, writing Galt's speech and it would prove to be the climax of her intellectual life as well as the book. It is the basis for the philosophy of Objectivism.

With the speech complete, Ayn began submitting the completed portions of the new novel to publishers. Bobbs-Merrill, the publisher of *The Fountainhead*, had an option on the book, but demanded cuts in the long manuscript. Ayn refused to discuss the alterations and the option expired. Given the sales of *The Fountainhead*, almost every major publisher was interested in publishing Ayn's new novel. She signed with Random House for a $50,000 advance and, in March 1957, delivered the finished manuscript. It was dedicated to Frank O'Connor and Nathaniel Branden.

Ayn was not prepared for the response to *Atlas Shrugged* when it was published in October 1957, almost thirteen years after she had begun outlining it. She had been reading the book to the Collective for years and received unified acclaim in return. The majority of the nation's book critics, on the other hand, were not as enamored with her work, and hardly anyone else was interested in publicly supporting a book that savaged almost every one of American society's institutions. The negative reaction, and, perhaps, the birth of the book that had occupied her for so long, depressed Ayn and stifled her sexual affair with Nathaniel, though their close friendship remained intact.

Sales were a different story. In a replay of *The Fountainhead*, the reading public embraced the book and its story of the strike by John Galt and the rest of society's prime movers. And, like *The Fountainhead*, sales grew steadily until hundreds of thousands and then millions of copies had been sold.

The Objectivist Explosion

There is an important difference between the post-publication periods of *The Fountainhead*'s and *Atlas Shrugged*. Ayn now had the energetic support of Nathaniel Branden and the rest of the Collective. Where previously the author had used the media simply as a vehicle for publicizing her books, her followers now urged her to begin using the media to promote her philosophy (which some called Randism, but Ayn insisted be labeled Objectivism). The writer was turning into a philosophic leader.

In January 1958, Nathaniel set up the Nathaniel Branden Institute (NBI) and a twenty-lecture course titled "Basic Principles of Objectivism."[4] Ayn approved all of the materials and by this time was referring to Nathaniel as her "intellectual heir." He was also designated her legal heir and was named to inherit all of Ayn and Frank's assets after their deaths.

The first course, held in a hotel meeting room, drew twenty-eight students. Soon they were being held twice a year and drawing 160 students. Nathaniel expanded the course offerings according to the demand. Associate lecturers (including Barbara Branden, Alan Greenspan, and Leonard Peikoff, among others) were teaching thinking skills, economics, and the history of philosophy from the Objectivist perspective. Ayn was also making regular appearances at the lectures, usually answering questions at the end of sessions. Ayn and Frank, the Brandens, and NBI were inextricably linked. All were housed in the same apartment building; they were living and working together.

Stimulated by book sales, Ayn's media appearances and speeches, and NBI, the Objectivist movement enjoyed fast growth. The entire operation was run by members of the Collective. The popularity of her ideas helped Ayn recover from her depression and her social circle expanded. The founders of the Libertarian movement joined with the Collective and she began an intellectual relationship with philosophy professor John Hospers.

In 1962, Random House published *Who Is Ayn Rand?* by Nathaniel and Barbara Branden, a worshipful analysis of Ayn's books and life that embarrasses both authors today. Ayn was especially popular on college campuses, where Ayn Rand clubs began to form and expand. In 1963, Portland,

Oregon's Lewis and Clark College granted her an honorary doctorate degree. By 1965, NBI had expanded into eighty other cities through the sale of taped lectures.

Although Ayn planned a new novel, it would never be written. In 1959, she revised *We the Living* for Random House and it became available for the first time since the 1930s. In 1961, Random House published *For the New Intellectual,* a collection of the philosophical speeches excerpted from her fiction. Ayn's energy went into speech writing and articles, produced mainly for *The Objectivist Newsletter* and its predecessor, *The Objectivist,* which she published in partnership with Nathaniel. In 1964 and 1966, two collections of those articles, *The Virtue of Selfishness* and *Capitalism: The Unknown Ideal,* were published.

Unhappily, as Objectivism spread, so did the authoritarianism and intolerance of its inner circle. Members who questioned the philosophy or decisions of Ayn or the Brandens often found themselves excommunicated from the group. The Saturday night sessions in Ayn's apartment would often degenerate into prolonged attacks on flaws in the thinking of specific members. Students at NBI who didn't phrase questions properly were verbally attacked in class. Ayn also broke with Random House, the most responsive publisher she had ever had, because in the wake of the assassination of President Kennedy, it would not publish, as part of a collection of her speeches, one that included a political analysis likening the altruism of Kennedy's New Frontier to Nazi Germany.

Objectivism was beginning to look more like a cult than

a philosophical movement. In a memoir of his relationship with Ayn, Nathaniel wrote:

> There were implicit premises in our world to which everyone in our circle subscribed. We transmitted these to our students at NBI. These were the premises:
>
> · Ayn Rand is the greatest human being that has ever lived.
> · *Atlas Shrugged* is the greatest human achievement in the history of the world.
> · Ayn Rand, by virtue of her philosophical genius, is the supreme arbiter in any issue pertaining to what is rational, moral, or appropriate to man's life on earth.

His list goes on for four more points that tie the students' personal virtue to their position on Rand and her work, link personal admiration of Rand to Objectivism, require similar devotion to Branden himself, and finally, ground all of the premises in reason and logic. Branden concludes, "Perhaps we were not a cult in the literal, dictionary sense of the word, but there was certainly a cultish aspect to our world…."[5]

Outwardly, the Objectivism movement was booming. By 1967, twenty-five thousand students graduated from NBI and more than 20,000 people subscribed to *The Objectivist*. NBI had opened its own publishing company as well as a book service dedicated to printing and selling texts aligned with Objectivism. Nathaniel even founded the NBI Theater to produce plays, the first of which was to be a stage adaptation of *The Fountainhead*. But internally, cult or not, the movement had become a time bomb.

THE BREAK AND AYN RAND'S DECLINE

The explosive core of the Objectivist movement was Ayn's affair with Nathaniel. In 1964, at age fifty-nine, she tried to rekindle the sexual element of their relationship. Unknown to Ayn, Nathaniel was already in the midst of another extramarital affair, this time with Patrecia Scott, a married woman and student of Objectivism, who was ten years younger than he.

After several months, Nathaniel admitted the affair to his wife, Barbara, and the couple formally separated, though their working relationship remained intact. At the same time, he resisted Ayn's attempts to reintroduce sex into their relationship, blaming his feelings about his ruined marriage. The result was ludicrous scenes in which Ayn advised Barbara to mend her marriage so Ayn could resume her love affair with Barbara's husband. This went on until 1967, when Nathaniel claimed he would not continue their sexual liaisons because of their age difference. Ayn still held on, now trying to help Nathaniel over his supposed mental barriers. Incredibly, this phase continued for another year.

In August 1968, Barbara finally forced Nathaniel to tell Ayn the truth. The resulting explosion came as no surprise to the Brandens. Nathaniel was instantly stripped of his authority and banished from the ranks of Objectivism. Neither he nor Ayn admitted the real cause of what came to be called simply "the break" to the shocked members of the Collective or the public. (Ayn never would.) Nathaniel resigned, saying in his final address to the staff of NBI and *The Objectivist,* "I have taken actions I know to be wrong. I have failed to practice the principles I taught to all of you. Ayn is fully within her moral rights in severing our relationship."[6]

Perversely, Ayn forgave Barbara for not informing her of Nathaniel's affair. But then, a few days later, Barbara was also exiled for questioning Ayn's increasingly vengeful treatment of her ex-husband. On Ayn's instructions, NBI was completely shut down. Nathaniel gave Ayn his 50 percent share in *The Objectivist* without payment. As Ayn demanded, most of the Collective cut off all contact with the Brandens, including members of their family and friends. Soon after, Nathaniel and Patrecia relocated to the West Coast, as did Barbara and her lover, a former NBI student named Robert Berole. For all intents and purposes, the formal Objectivist movement was dead.

The break took a heavy toll on Ayn, but she continued publishing *The Objectivist* until September 1971, when she replaced it with a new, shorter newsletter, *The Ayn Rand Letter.* Two more collections of articles were published as books:

The Romantic Manifesto in 1969 and *The New Left: The Anti-Industrial Revolution* in 1971.

Even though Ayn never allowed her name to be associated with a formal organization again, members of the Collective continued to lecture about Objectivism and she approved their materials. Leonard Peikoff, Barbara's cousin, remained loyal to Ayn and she eventually named him her new intellectual and legal heir.

In 1973, Ayn was astounded to receive a letter from her youngest sister, Nora, still living in Russia. (In 1946, Ayn learned that her parents had died of illnesses under Stalin. Her sister Natasha was killed during a World War II air raid.) Nora and her husband came for a visit that same year and Ayn prepared an apartment for the couple in her building, hoping they would stay. Instead, Ayn and Nora found they had nothing in common and soon were not speaking to each other. Incomprehensibly to Ayn, Nora returned to Russia six weeks after she arrived.

Ill-health and advancing age began to take their toll in the 1970s. In 1974, Ayn, a heavy smoker whose trademark cigarette holder was never far from her grasp, was diagnosed with cancer and the lesion on her lung was removed. Frank suffered from arterial sclerosis, memory loss, and disorientation. Ayn recovered, but Frank's health grew progressively worse.

Ayn wrote less and less after her illness. She stopped publishing her newsletter in 1976 and the last of the original Collective, except for Leonard, had dropped away by 1979. Ayn's book, *Introduction to Objectivist Epistemology*, a collection of her philosophical articles from the mid-1960s, was published that year. The book prompted a flurry of media appearances and under Leonard's direction, a new periodical, *The Intellectual Activist*, was founded.

Frank died in November 1979. He was eighty-two years old and had been married to Ayn for fifty years. Ayn wrote a few more articles and planned another collection, but she never truly recovered from the loss. In November 1981, she was enticed to give a speech in New Orleans by the opportunity to travel there in a sumptuous, private railcar. The speech was a great success but the effort seems to have seriously weakened her. Ayn became ill on the way back to New York. She did not recover, dying of heart failure at home on March 6, 1982, at the age of 77.

Ayn's influence did not end with her death. Leonard, in his role as Ayn's intellectual heir, has been actively editing and publishing her writings, including selections of her journals and letters, ever since. In 1985, with funding from a wealthy businessman, the nonprofit Ayn Rand Institute (ARI) was founded under Leonard's control and the Ayn Rand Archives were established. It is the official headquarters of Objectivism.

The ideological rigidity of the Collective continues to this day and members of the inner circle who do not toe the intellectual line are still excommunicated. One result of that has been the splintering of Objectivism as exiled members form their own organizations, such as the Institute for Objectivist Studies (IOS), which was founded in 1990 and attracts former outcasts of the movement. ARI treats Ayn's Objectivism as a complete and total philosophy that can only be studied and lived as it was written; IOS sees Ayn's work as a foundation to be interpreted and built upon.

Internal squabbles and cracks in infrastructure aside, the foundation of Objectivism remains the strong and enduring interest in Ayn Rand and her thinking. Her life continues to intrigue and fascinate those who come into contact with her works. More than 400,000 people still buy her books every year. And, the Objectivist philosophy, the subject of the next chapter, is gaining a secure place in the academic arena and is increasingly taught in college-level philosophy courses.

3

A
PHILOSOPHY
FOR
LIVING

AYN RAND WAS AN unlikely philosopher. While most modern philosophers were presenting their ideas in peer-reviewed professional journals, she was writing best-selling novels of ideas that entertained on a grand scale. While most philosophers were teaching in classrooms, she was lecturing Johnny Carson on late night television and arguing with the audience of *The Phil Donahue Show*. While most philosophers were analyzing the ideas of long-dead thinkers, such as Plato and Aristotle, she was critiquing the current actions of the world's governments.

Rand shoved the issues of philosophy into the mainstream of society and opened the debate to the general public. Even those critical of Objectivism admit that, in doing so, she made philosophy matter in a way that only a select group of philosophers have been able to match. Philosopher William O'Neill wrote: "Whatever else Miss Rand may have achieved, she continues to serve as a useful intellectual catalyst in a society which frequently suffers from philosophical 'tired blood.'"[1]

The extent of Ayn Rand's philosophical achievement is the subject of ongoing and often bitter debate. Committed Objectivists claim that she created nothing less than a complete and integrated system for living on earth. Those less enamored with Rand declare that she said little or nothing that is original, creating instead a cult of personality. If there is an exact answer, it lies somewhere between the two extremes.

Rand herself fostered much of the acrimony surrounding Objectivism by using words as weapons. She redefined emotionally charged words and applied them to describe her ideas. She then became expert at using them to create sound bytes that shocked audiences unfamiliar with their context: Altruism was evil; religion was immoral; selfishness was good. Anyone who did not agree with her statements either did not know any better or was an enemy, evil and irrational. Words and the way Rand wielded them created instant adversaries and made the Objectivist movement confrontational in nature.

The personal behavior of Rand and her followers also damaged the reputation of Objectivism. By holding themselves up as perfect examples of the philosophy, Rand and the members of the Collective linked Objectivism to their personal foibles. By demanding complete obedience to its scripture and exiling those unable to deliver it, the Objectivist movement became a dictatorship. Critics simply combined Objectivism and the behavior of its adherents into a single target and took pot shots at the resulting hypocrisies.

Finally, Objectivism tends to be obscured by the fact that Rand herself never wrote a full, nonfiction treatise describing the philosophy in its entirety. The closest she came to a complete exposition was the sixty-page radio speech delivered by John Galt in *Atlas Shrugged*, but to get a full picture of Objectivism in Rand's own words, one must extract it from her novels, lectures, speeches, and articles. (It wasn't until 1991 that a full treatment became available when Rand's heir, Leonard Peikoff, completed *Objectivism: The Philosophy of Ayn Rand*.)

Nevertheless, behind all of the fireworks and the misconceptions, Objectivism remains a philosophy worth understanding. It is firmly grounded in reality; Objectivism is practical. Further, it champions individual rights, celebrates reason, and posits a world of unlimited opportunity to anyone who cares to work for it. Objectivism is a "philosophy for living."

PHILOSOPHY AND ITS COMPONENTS

Rand knew that the phrase "philosophy for living" was redundant, but she used it because she knew that in the minds of most people, the discipline of philosophy was an arcane word game that appeared to have little relevance in their daily lives. In the Objectivist view, nothing could be further from the truth.

In March 1974, when Rand spoke at the United States Military Academy at West Point, she began by asking the cadets to picture themselves as astronauts whose rocket has crashed on an unexplored alien world. "When you regain consciousness and find that you are not hurt badly," she said, "the first three questions in your mind would be: Where am I? How I can discover it? What should I do?"[2] These are the same questions that philosophy seeks to answer, Rand explained.

Philosophy is the study of reality or, as the dictionary defines it, "the investigation of the causes and laws underlying reality."[3] The answers that we uncover during that investigation become the foundation on which we base our actions and our lives. They can be answers that we discover for ourselves, as Objectivism requires, or they can be answers that others propose and we accept on faith, such as Christianity. Further, we may or may not be conscious of the answers we live by. For instance, knee-jerk emotional responses are often based on undiscovered subconscious beliefs.

The study of all reality is a huge topic, so philosophy has been broken down into manageable components. The components that Rand addressed with Objectivism are metaphysics, epistemology, ethics, politics, and esthetics, and she strictly ordered them on the basis of their priority. Metaphysics explains the nature of the universe and the individual's relationship to it. Epistemology explores the nature of human knowledge. Ethics studies the proper behavior of humans. Politics, the way in which humans live together. And esthetics, the nature of beauty or art. Together, they add up to a worldview or, as Rand said, "a philosophy for living on earth."

She decided on the name Objectivism in 1956, just before Nathaniel Branden began the initial lecture series aimed at describing it. Rand chose Objectivism because her metaphysics, epistemology, and ethics were built on what she called objective values. As we will soon see, and in opposition to many other philosophies, she maintained that an objective reality exists, that we are capable of knowing it, and that we can base and judge our actions on that knowledge.

In 1957, a few months before Random House released *Atlas Shrugged,* Ayn Rand was invited to a meeting of the publisher's sales staff. Looking for a succinct statement to help him sell the book, one of the salespeople asked her to sum up her philosophy while standing on one foot. "Metaphysics—objective reality; Epistemology—reason; Ethics—self-interest; Politics—capitalism," she unhesitatingly reeled off with one foot in the air.[4] In the 1960s, after Rand had formalized her opinions on the arts, she could have completed the list by adding "Esthetics—romantic realism."

Rand had described the primary components of Objectivism in a single breath, but it is doubtful that the salesman sold many copies of *Atlas Shrugged* based on her answer. A basic understanding of what each word means requires a short overview of her thinking in each area.[5]

METAPHYSICS—OBJECTIVE REALITY

Metaphysics establishes the broad vision of the playing field on which people live out their lives. It seeks to define what is out there or, as Rand told West Point's cadets, "Where am I?"

The knowable, rational universe that Objectivist metaphysics describes is based on three axioms (self-evident, irreducible facts) that explain the fundamental nature of the universe and everything in it. They are the axioms of existence, consciousness, and identity.

"Existence exists" is the statement with which Rand started explaining the nature of reality. Simply, the axiom of existence says that things exist outside of our consciousness and independently of our thoughts. The universe is not something we dreamed up, declared Rand, and whether or not we choose to acknowledge it, it is real.

The axiom of identity says that each thing that exists has its own unchangeable identity. A chair will not change simply because we conjure an image of it as a table. It is still a chair and we can depend on that fact.

And, finally, the act of realizing that something exists and that each thing has an identity is a direct demonstration of the axiom of consciousness. It says we are able to perceive that which exists; we are conscious beings.

Rand used the three axioms to develop some important conclusions about the nature of reality. For instance, the axiom and primacy of existence (the fact that things exist prior to a consciousness of them) demolishes the idea of a created universe. Thus, Objectivists are, by definition, rationalists. They reject magic, mysticism, and philosophies that require faith. They are atheists. The axioms of existence and identity preclude the ability to contradict the fixed nature of things. Objectivists respect reality and work within its boundaries. And the axioms of existence, identity, and consciousness combine to eliminate fundamental conflicts in the universe and in man's nature. Objectivists see man as a unified being in harmony with the universe. Conflicts are not natural, but are errors in thinking that can be corrected.

Rand's metaphysics describes an objective reality that exists without the need for a supreme commander or judge. It is a noncontradictory universe; there are no metaphysical conflicts between the things in it. Human beings are a natural and harmonious part of Rand's reality, and they, too, live in it without fundamental conflict.

EPISTEMOLOGY—REASON

Epistemology, the next building block in philosophy, establishes how humans understand and relate to the metaphysical reality. It answers the second question asked by Rand's hypothetical astronaut, "How can I discover it?"

Rand separated the process of gaining knowledge into two components: sense perception and reason. People, said Rand, receive objective information directly through their senses and then interpret it, either rightly or wrongly, using the faculty of reason. Because of this, our senses are our primary source of knowledge.

In exploring reason, Rand made a subtle argument involving concepts, definitions, and essences, and the relationships among them. Her conclusion was that reason is the only way that humans are able to interpret the information they receive from their senses, and that reason can provide objective knowledge. This means that we live in a knowable universe and how well we live in it is determined by how well we develop our ability to reason.

With the power of reason established, Objectivism turns its attention to the owners of reason. Rand argues that like every other living thing human beings are goal-oriented and their most important goal is life itself—that is, their survival.

Our main means of survival, she continued, is our ability

to think—that is, reason. But how much and how well we think is a matter of choice. People, said Rand, are volitional creatures. Individuals are not forced to think, nor is the degree to which they think mandated.

Rand's epistemology proclaims that people are, first and foremost, free and independent beings. If they choose, they can, through the use of their senses and their ability to reason, objectively know and judge reality. Or, they can choose not to think. The degree to which people exercise their mental abilities determines how much they achieve, how successful they become, and how well they will live their lives.

Ethics—Self-Interest

Ethics, the study of rules of proper human behavior, is the next logical issue in Objectivism. It establishes the proper human goals and the actions required to achieve them. For Rand's astronaut, that means that after determining where he is and how he can know it, the next important question to answer is, "What should I do?"

In Objectivist thinking, the goals which people pursue are their *values*. Rand says that because humans are able choose their values, their ethical values are, by definition, their morality. Since an individual's life is the most important goal for that person, it is also the ultimate moral value. And, finally, since life is the ultimate goal and happiness is the result of achieving goals, pursuing your life and being happy do not conflict. They are two sides of the same coin.

Rand breaks down the ultimate value of life into three component values: reason, purpose, and self-esteem. As stated above, humans have to think in order to survive; they must pursue reason. Humans have to define and decide the values worth pursuing; they must have purpose. And humans must accept the value of their lives and their own minds; they must have self-esteem. Together, reason, purpose, and self-esteem support life and form the three-sided pyramid that Rand labeled *rational self-interest*.

Objectivist ethics goes a step further by answering the question of how people can achieve these values. Rand identified seven virtues (or behaviors) that we can adopt toward that end. The first three correspond directly to the three Objectivist values; they are rationality, productiveness, and pride. The remaining virtues support the pursuit of reason; they are independence, integrity, honesty, and justice.

The Objectivist ethics are where the rubber hits the road. Rand upholds the primacy of the individual and rejects as illogical and immoral any system that puts the rights of society or any collective of people over the rights of individuals. But she does not say that individuals should choose goals or behaviors at random. Instead, she offers people values and virtues (goals and specific actions) that are consistent with the Objectivist worldview. If individuals accept and pursue these goals, they are acting in rational self-interest, which does not conflict with other people acting from the same ethical system.

Politics—Capitalism

Politics is a specialized branch of philosophy that studies how humans should live together. Rand never fully developed her political philosophy, but she did articulate some basic principles. She started by asserting that politics must follow directly from the values and virtues of individual ethics. It also had to be consistent with the metaphysics and epistemology on which it is based. The proper political system could not contradict any of the philosophy that went before it.

Since Objectivist ethics declare the primacy of the individual and of reason, physical force is outlawed. Reason is destroyed if people can be compelled to act against their interests. Rand agreed with America's founding fathers that society must be based on the rights of individuals. These rights start with the right to life itself and extend to the right to freedom, property, and the pursuit of happiness. Rand declared that the political system's only proper role is to protect individual rights. For Objectivists, government should serve no other purpose.

The only political philosophy that fits these requirements is capitalism. Rand, however, was not advocating capitalism as it exists in practice, but capitalism in a purer form. In laissez-faire capitalism, people live and work together by mutual consent and for their mutual benefit. All property is privately owned and all products and services are traded for. The government protects the rights of individuals through a legal system or, if needed, through the use of properly sanctioned force.

Objectivism's politics is opposed to established political philosophies such as conservatism and liberalism. An Objectivist government would have very limited powers relating solely to the protection of rights. It would not provide education or social welfare nor would it control the economy in any way. Based on her fundamental restructuring of existing political systems, Rand defined Objectivists as radicals for capitalism.

ESTHETICS—ROMANTIC REALISM

Like politics, the study of the nature of art and beauty, or esthetics, is a specialized branch of philosophy and is built on the metaphysics, epistemology, and ethics that precede it. It is not surprising that Rand spent a significant amount of time and energy examining esthetics. As a writer of novels, stories, and plays for stage and screen, she was intimately concerned with the philosophy that supported her creative efforts.

Art, according to Rand, is an emotional activity that, like emotion, is ruled by reason. The artist is expressing his philosophical view of the world — his *sense of life* — in a physical form. The people who experience the finished work respond based on their sense of life.

In contradiction to many art philosophers, Rand declared that art can judged, and she judged it harshly. For instance, an artwork that does not express a recognizable worldview, such as an Abstract Expressionist painting, is not actually art at all in the Objectivist view. Many of the most acclaimed works of Modern art were worthless according to Rand. Likewise, a great book is one that communicates the writer's worldview using the highest level of technical and creative excellence in that endeavor. James Joyce and Thomas Wolfe need not apply in Rand's view.

Objectivist esthetics support Romantic Realism, which according to Rand, envisions mankind's highest potential. Great art, therefore follows the major themes of the Objectivist philosophy. It expertly and overtly expresses the openness of the universe to human achievement and a heroic portrayal of man.

In part one, we have explored the major events and influences in Ayn Rand's life and the principal elements of Objectivism, the philosophy she created and championed. From this foundation, we can start to examine why Ayn

Rand and her ideas matter to businesspeople. In part two, we will take Objectivism to work and examine the impact that the values and virtues of Objectivist ethics can make on a business career.

2

Randian

Work

4

VALUES AND VIRTUES FOR BUSINESSPEOPLE

WHY DO YOU WORK? On the surface, it sounds like a simple question, but there are many possible answers and combinations of answers. Perhaps, you work to support yourself and your family, to earn the respect of other people, or to experience the satisfaction of a job well done. Perhaps, the answer appears obvious—you work because that is what people do. Whatever your answers to the question are, they illuminate your philosophical beliefs or as Ayn Rand liked to say, your *premises*.

Rand answered the question "Why do you work?" by creating Howard Roark. In 1943, Rand brought Roark naked, but far from crying, into the world. In the opening scene of *The Fountainhead*, Roark, wearing only his orange-red hair, dives from a granite cliff into a lake. He has just been expelled from the school where he has spent three years studying architecture and he is happy.

From the beginning of *The Fountainhead*, it is obvious that Roark, to paraphrase Thoreau, is marching to the beat of a different drummer. The career path that the architect follows appears contradictory to the outside world. Even though he is on the edge of bankruptcy and struggling to establish his own practice, Roark turns down a lucrative and prestigious architectural project. Offered a job in a highly regarded architectural firm, he chooses to work in a stone quarry instead. And yet there is an internal consistency to Rand's famous hero.

That consistency derives from Roark's beliefs. He knows that if he accepts the job at the highly regarded firm or the lucrative assignment, he would be forced to compromise his principles and code of ethics. He will not make such a choice. "His whole *philosophy:* pride in oneself, confidence in oneself, placing one's life and fate above all, but only the *kind* of life one wishes," is how Rand described the character in a sketch in her writing journal in 1936.[1]

Rand's philosophical tenets were not yet completely developed when she created Roark, but he remains her most fully drawn version of the ideal man. Roark lives and works for himself. He chooses his own goals and is willing to labor extraordinarily hard and long to achieve them. He knows his ethical principles and will not violate them either for others or in pursuit of his own ends. He is independent and true to himself.

Interestingly, for all of his independence and his convictions, Roark is never dogmatic. He seeks to understand the reasoning and motives of the book's other characters. He will not, however, accept the boundaries or values of other people or society in general until he has compared them to his own and they have proven sound. Nor do the reasoning or motives of others necessarily concern Roark. He will accept assignments as long as he is given the freedom to pursue them on his own terms.

Rand uses Roark to deliver her first major statement of rational egoism. At the end of *The Fountainhead,* the architect is on trial for blowing up Cortland Homes, a public housing development that he agreed to design without financial payment, but with one stipulation: His final plans cannot be altered in any way. When it is not built as agreed and with no legal recourse, he destroys the project.

In lieu of a formal defense and acting as his own counsel, Roark makes a single personal statement in which he argues that his contract was violated and so his destruction of the results of that contract are fully within his rights. The speech is based on the idea that a human being's highest value and responsibility is to his own life; that the needs of the individual are more important than the needs of any collective society. The jury agrees and Roark is exonerated.

Selfishness As the Prime Mover

In Roark's speech, Rand made a strong argument for a morality based on selfishness. She pegs all human progress and civilization itself to the behavior of egoists. She calls these people *selfish,* but not in the normal sense of the word.

We usually think of selfish people as concerned with their own interests to the detriment of the people around them. Selfishness, it is commonly held, is a human flaw. We are taught by our governmental, educational, and religious institutions that selfish behavior is improper and harmful to society.

Rand redefined the word *selfish* and, in doing so, turned the common conception of the word on its head. Selfishness does not preclude a concern for other people in her meaning of the word. Rather, just as passengers on a plane are instructed to put on their own oxygen masks first in case of an emergency, it simply requires that concern for yourself and your life precede concern for others. People must first serve themselves. It is their moral duty. There is an internal logic to Rand's position: If you do not provide for your own life, how will you provide for others?

For Rand, any philosophy based on altruism, that suggested that individuals concern themselves with the needs of other before their own needs, was illogical and ludicrous. Carried out to its logical conclusions, people would be obligated to stop working so others would have jobs; stop eating so others would have food; kill themselves so others could live. Altruism and selfless behavior were immoral to Rand.

Although Objectivists seem to enjoy the shock value of identifying committed altruists, such as Mother Theresa, as immoral people, neither Rand nor her philosophical followers are in direct opposition to philanthropy and charitable works. If, after you provide your own needs, you wish to serve others, go right ahead, said Rand. The choice of how you spend the fruits of your labor is your own, as long as it does not conflict with your own well-being.

In Roark's speech to the jury, Ayn Rand tied her definition of selfishness to a force that she calls the "Prime Mover."[2] It is the energy, she explains, that drives the world's creators, who, in turn, produce all human progress. This force is internally generated. It cannot be imposed or demanded. "The creators were not selfless," declares Rand through Roark. "It is the whole secret of their power—that it was self-sufficient, self-motivated, self-generated."[3]

Who are these creators? In her fiction, Rand fashioned characters such as Roark and John Galt and the other strikers in *Atlas Shrugged* to illustrate her concept of the internally driven person. In her nonfiction, she specified the innovators and empire builders of the Industrial Age, such as Henry Ford, who pioneered the moving assembly line, and Andrew Carnegie, who created Big Steel. Today, Objectivists point to the entrepreneurs of the Information Age, such as Michael

Dell, who built an industry giant around the direct marketing of personal computers, and Bill Gates, who founded the world's most powerful software company. In Rand's eyes, they are all producers, people who create new products, services, and processes. They create wealth by adding value to the world at large.

Rand's concept of selfishness fits into the larger context of the Objectivist philosophy and her selfish prime movers are governed by its logic. Like Roark, all of these achievers live for their own goals and by their own code of behavior. They are driven by self-interest, but it is not unbridled. Their self-interest is a rational self-interest, and it is directed toward achieving three specific goals. These goals, known as the Objectivist values, are Rand's answer to the question: "Why do you work?" We work to achieve our highest potential of our lives. "To live," she wrote in Galt's radio speech, "man must hold three things as the supreme and ruling values of his life: Reason — Purpose — Self-esteem."[4]

Reason

If you believe that success in business and life is more than fate or sheer luck, then Objectivism teaches you that reason is the only basis for understanding and attaining it. Reason, as we saw in chapter three, is the method by which humans know the world. Rand identified reason as the primary value from which the other values and virtues of Objectivism flow. It is, according to Leonard Peikoff, "one of the central concepts in the philosophy of Ayn Rand. The whole of Objectivism amounts to the injunction: 'Follow reason.' "[5]

For prime movers, adopting reason as a value means an unwavering commitment to reality. They understand that if they do not base their visions and efforts on the conditions in the real world they cannot hope to succeed. In fact, their success often rests upon their ability to understand reality better than their contemporaries can. For example, FedEx founder Fred Smith received a grade of 'C' on college paper that described his concept for the overnight air service. His professor wrote, " …in order to earn better than a 'C,' the idea must be feasible."[6]

The adoption of reason also means the prime movers' unwavering commitment to their ability to think, to the use of their own minds. They accept the Objectivist logic that they live in a knowable world and that they are capable of understanding it. Thomas Edison, arguably the most prolific inventor in history, built a "creativity factory" dedicated to the premise that people could innovate on demand. It was in that Menlo Park complex that Edison steadfastly tested thousands of different materials before finding the right filament for his electric lightbulb.

It should be obvious by now that the pursuit of reason is not a philosophical ideal. Like Objectivism itself, it is firmly grounded in the practical. Reason, said Rand, is the source of life. People cannot survive without pursuing knowledge and they certainly cannot prosper without using their minds. Conversely, the better that they understand reality and the better they become at using their own brains, the more successful they will become.

Purpose

The successful achievement of any major life or career goal requires a long-term focus and an intensity of energy. In other words, it requires a purpose. "A central purpose serves to integrate all the other concerns of a man's life," said Rand. "In order to be in control of your life, you have to have a purpose—a productive purpose."[7]

Rand defined the primary purpose of prime movers as *productive work.* In business terms, productive work is creative work that uses reason to create valuable new products and services that, in turn, result in the generation of wealth. Walt Disney is a good example of a man whose purpose was productive work. Disney, who holds the record for the most Oscars awarded to any individual. He released the first cartoons with sound and color, and the first feature-length cartoons. In doing so, he elevated the lowly cartoon into an art form. Not content to stop there, he brought his animations to life and created Disneyland and, with it, the theme park industry.

Prime movers relentlessly pursue their multi-billion dollar purpose. Purpose is long-term value and its achievement may well stretch over an entire lifetime. Rand's life story is a vivid example of purpose in action. She traversed the thousands of miles, bridged the language barriers and the radical cultural differences between Leningrad and Hollywood in pursuit of her purpose. Then, she worked against all odds for another two decades before producing *The Fountainhead*.

As with reason, the establishment and achievement of a productive purpose is an eminently practical task. Purpose allows us to define the direction of our lives. It enables us to evaluate and decide on the best choices we can make for our careers and lives.

Self-Esteem

The final requirement for the achievement of a successful life and career is a firm belief in one's own worth. Rand defined self-esteem as an individual's "inviolate certainty that his mind is competent to think and his person is worthy of happiness, which means: is worthy of living."[8]

Self-esteem gives prime movers the confidence they need to rely on their own ability to reason. "Since the self is the mind," writes Leonard Peikoff, "self-esteem is mind esteem."[9]

Michael Dell founded Dell Computer on the confidence in his own judgment that selling PCs directly to customers was a viable basis for starting a company. "I didn't ask for permission or approval," says Dell, who was at the time an eighteen-year-old college student. "I just went ahead and did it."[10]

Dell was certainly not encouraged to pursue a career in direct computer sales. In the early days, his parents were very upset that he was straying from his pre-Med coursework. Even after he convinced them by selling up to $80,000 worth of computers per month while still in school, no one else put much credence in the new business model. It was self-esteem — Dell's belief in himself and the results he was generating that supported his ambition.

The value of self-esteem brings with it the ability to withstand the pressure of opposing opinions and viewpoints. It also gives the prime mover the courage to move beyond the boundaries of convention. In the late 1960s anyone who had said that they planned to enter the mature, capital-intensive steel industry would have been ostracized. Then, Ken Iverson, the creator of Nucor Steel, re-envisioned the entire concept of a steel mill. With a $6 million bank loan, he built the first "mini-mill" as a way to reduce the costs of the steel his company needed for its manufacturing processes. The Nucor mill utilized electric arc furnaces and scrap iron, and radically reduced the costs of producing steel. It was a bet-the-company gamble and it paid off. Nucor's new mills revolutionized the industry at a time when no one else believed that you could compete with Big Steel. Today, Nucor is one of the world's largest steelmakers itself.

Self-esteem gives us trust in the power of our minds and the strength to stand behind our ideas and beliefs. As Ayn Rand said, before you can value anything or anyone else, you must first value yourself. Self-esteem is the basis for the ability to value your life and your accomplishments.

Achieving the Objectivist Values

Once Rand established reason, purpose, and self-esteem as the goals of our lives and work, she asked the next natural question: How can we achieve those goals? Her answer to that question was the Objectivist virtues, seven actions or behaviors that people can adopt to reach their highest potential.

Rand's first recorded attempt at describing a set of behaviors for individualists appears in her working journals. After *The Fountainhead* was released, the author proposed a short nonfiction book describing the philosophy underlying the popular novel. In August 1943, her publisher, Bobbs-Merrill, agreed to publish the book, tentatively titled *The Moral Basis of Individualism,* and Rand set to work. In a September journal entry, she described nine primary virtues that support independence of mind.[11] The book, which Rand originally estimated would take a month to complete, was never finished, but the beginnings of a set of Objectivist virtues was established.

Ten years later, in her working journal for *Atlas Shrugged*, Rand took another stab at defining the virtues. She was outlining John Galt's radio speech, the basis for Objectivism, when she listed six qualities as "the virtues of the Life Morality."[12] By the time the book was published in 1957, the virtues had evolved once again. Now, there were seven actions for achieving the values in one's life and work: rationality, independence, integrity, honesty, justice, productiveness, and pride.

The virtues are, Rand explained, the actions that lead to the achievement of values. Three of the virtues correspond directly to the Objectivist values. Reason is achieved through rationality. Purpose is achieved through productiveness. Self-esteem is achieved through pride. The remaining four virtues—independence, integrity, honesty, and justice—are derivative values supporting rationality, which Rand pinpointed as the primary virtue.

Rand's virtues offer a set of actions for getting the highest return from our lives. If you reduce the context to business, they also offer a set of practices for getting the most value from our work. In the next seven chapters, we will explore the Objectivist virtues in greater detail and examine what they mean for businesspeople.

5

RATIONALITY

AYN RAND PUT RATIONALITY first on her list of seven life-sustaining virtues. In Objectivism, rationality, or the act of thinking, is the foundational element of life. You can refuse to use your mind, but the logical result of shutting down your brain is death. Conversely, the more you use your ability to think, the more you can achieve with your life.

Rand worshipped reason and rationality was her form of prayer. She constructed the philosophy of Objectivism upon the foundation of reason and she wrote novels in which the heroes were thinking people. *Atlas Shrugged* was Rand's paean to reason and rationality. "The actual hero of *Atlas Shrugged* is: man's mind," wrote Nathaniel Branden. "The novel dramatizes what reason is, how it functions and what happens to the world when the men of the mind—the men who create motors, railroads, metals, philosophies, and symphonies—refuse to be martyred by the rule of irrationalism."[1]

In *Atlas Shrugged*, Rand portrays rationality as an inexorable force and the most powerful weapon in the strikers' arsenal. The strike is itself a war against irrationality. It starts, the reader learns late in the novel, when the owners and employees at a company that manufactures motors vote to adopt a new work system. Using a communistic formula, all workers will contribute their best efforts, but the rewards of their work will be assigned based on individual needs. For one employee, a young engineer named John Galt, the vote provides the final break from a world that is increasingly controlled by what Rand calls "second-handers"—people who live on the achievements of others. Galt leaves the company, declaring, "I will stop the motor of the world."[2]

Rationality is the means by which Galt accomplishes his pledge. He uses reason to persuade society's prime movers to stop working. One by one, Galt convinces the world's greatest industrialists, artists, and thinkers to disappear. They leave behind the products of their minds, the businesses and ideas that they have created, but no one is capable of picking up the reins that they drop. As more and more producers abandon the world, the economy and the country itself begin to collapse.

Meanwhile, the strikers themselves relocate to a utopia hidden away in Colorado's Rocky Mountains nicknamed Galt's Gulch. Rand's brave new world is governed by what would become known as Objectivism and it depends on a strict adherence to reason and the power of rationality.

Rand used life in this Eden of individualism to provide a stark contrast to the collapsing outside world of *Atlas*

Shrugged. There are severe shortages of raw materials in the outside world, while inside Galt's Gulch, metals are efficiently extracted from the earth using innovative new advances in mining technology. Outside, power shortages and outages threaten to become permanent, while inside, oil is flowing from shale and a miraculous motor is generating electricity. Outside, rationality is being abandoned and inside, it is worshipped as the most valuable of all currencies. The winning philosophy quickly becomes obvious. With little physical action on the part of the strikers and less than two decades after Galt declares his intent, the outside world simply grinds to a halt. Eliminating rationality from the world does more than halt human progress; it reverses it.

Rationality Defined

Rationality is the act of using your ability to reason. "The virtue of *Rationality* means the recognition and acceptance of reason as one's only source of knowledge, one's only judge of values, and one's only guide to action," declared Rand in a speech at the University of Wisconsin.[3]

The idea that your own brain power is the best source of answers about how you should conduct your career may seem obvious, but a moment's reflection reveals that many people do not depend first and foremost on their own rationality. Many make choices based on the opinions of others. In business, they chase their customers and the latest trends and fads. Others base their choices on faith and emotion. They eschew action for good intentions and feelings and wait to see what the world will bring them. Still others avoid making any choices at all. They leave that to their bosses. To Rand, each of these is an evasion of the Objectivist commandment to practice rationality.

As the examples above suggest, rationality is a choice. People are not forced to act rationally. Barring physical shortcomings, they can use their brains to whatever extent they wish. By defining rationality as the foundational virtue of Objectivism, Rand emphasized how important it is for people to make the choice to think for themselves and not to live by the unconsidered dictates of others.

Rand did not suggest that it was easy to exercise the virtue of rationality, nor did she underestimate the difficulty of choosing it. She considered it a moral decision of the highest order and a heroic one at that. Her major fictional characters are often forced to stand up for their thinking against the combined onslaught of public opinion, governmental and institutional pressure, and the media. They win those battles, but the cost is always high. In her own life, Rand took a similarly uncompromising approach to her life and career. For better and sometimes for worse, she stood by her thinking.

Thinking rationally means acting rationally. To Rand, there was no separation between the mind and the body and likewise, there is no separation between knowing the right thing and doing it. Perhaps the greatest sin in Objectivism is knowing what is rationally correct, but not acting in support of that knowledge. Rand's greatest villains are characters that purposely subvert reason. They are truly evil.

So what does it mean to practice rationality on a day-to-day basis? For Objectivists, it means respecting reality, using the mind to its greatest extent, and taking responsibility for the results of that thinking.

Respecting Reality

Acting rationally requires the acceptance of and respect for objective reality. Reality, in Objectivism, is a hard fact and it exists apart from our dreams and desires. Our task is to understand that reality as best we can and never attempt to deny it.

Rand illustrated the critical need to respect reality in a memorable scene in *Atlas Shrugged* during which every passenger on the *Comet*, a transcontinental train, dies by suffocation. They are smothered when a coal-powered engine is used to pull them through an inadequately ventilated, eight-mile long tunnel. Among the dead is the politician who demanded that the train's schedule be kept without regard for the known risks. He refused to respect the reality of the situation and in doing so, set in motion a chain of events that killed everyone aboard the train except for a single member of the crew, and demolished a second train and the tunnel itself.

The *Comet* disaster is an imaginary one, but we can see the consequences of how well people respect reality in business every day. In 1996, Bill Gates belatedly and very publicly reinvented his own corporate strategy and reoriented Microsoft as an Internet company. With that act, he accepted the realities of the marketplace. Gates understood the fact that no matter what he wanted the future to look like, it was going to be Web-driven and that, if Microsoft were to continue to grow and prosper, it had to adjust itself to that reality.

If Gates had refused to recognize the reality of the business environment, Microsoft could easily have ended up like Iridium LLC. In 1987, Motorola decided to build and launch sixty-six satellites into a complex grid 420 miles above the earth and, in doing so, create the first global wireless telephone network. To accomplish this gargantuan task, it formed Iridium, a consortium of aerospace and communications companies that built rockets and satellites, cut deals with countries around the world, and raised and spent billions.

In 1998, within a few months of its targeted completion date, Iridium actually opened for business and started selling phone service anywhere on the planet. It was a triumph and a total disaster. In August 1999, less than a year after it opened for business, Iridium filed Chapter 11 bankruptcy. In late

2000, its satellite network was sold off for a half-penny on the dollar (or $25 million for a $5 billion investment).

What happened? In 1987, when Motorola first started batting around the idea of a global, satellite-based network, cell phones were rare. By 1994, there were 20 million cellular phone subscribers in the United States alone. And, in 1998, when Iridium was ready, there were close to a half billion global wireless subscribers. The rapid spread of cell phones shrank the need for Iridium's service until there was not enough demand left to support it. The leaders of the company evaded this reality. They refused to acknowledge that between 1987 and 1998 the market for their service had disappeared. Reality shut Iridium down.

A Fully Engaged Mind

The example of Iridium is also a good illustration of the need to fully engage reality throughout our careers. For Iridium, the market of 1987 was not the same market that existed more than a decade later. Unfortunately, the thinking on which the business was based was never updated to reflect the changing market.

Thinking, explained Rand, "is an actively sustained process of identifying one's impressions in conceptual terms, of integrating every event and every observation into a conceptual context, of grasping relationships, differences, similarities in one's perceptual material, and of abstracting them into new concepts, of drawing inferences, of making deductions, of reaching conclusions, of asking new questions and discovering new answers and expanding one's knowledge into an ever-growing sum."[4]

Rationality requires an intense pursuit of knowledge. When Rand declared that people have a choice to think or not think, she realized that human rationality is not as simple as a light switch, which is either on or off. Because we all use our ability to think in varying degrees, Rand emphasized the need to maximize the use of our minds. To accept rationality as a virtue is to make a commitment to as full and systematic a mental effort as we are able.

Rand also said that rationality requires a continuous effort. Thinking is not a part-time job. We cannot choose to think on Mondays, Wednesdays, and Fridays, but not on Tuesdays and Thursdays. Nor can we stop thinking at some arbitrary point in our lives. Rand's philosophy demands life-long learning.

In the 1990s, CEO Andrew Grove helped Intel gain a virtual monopoly in the global semiconductor market by insisting on a flat-out effort to cannibalize the company's own products. Grove forced Intel's engineers to design and build more powerful and speedier chips so quickly that competing companies were unable to mount an effective competitive attack. In essence, he demanded that the brains in the organization be used consistently and to their greatest capacity. As a result, Intel captured 80 percent of the semiconductor market and annual revenues grew from under $4 billion in 1990 to $29 billion in 1999.

Andy Grove put the mind power of Intel to work and enjoyed a long run of success, but practicing rationality over an entire career is a difficult and rarely accomplished task. For example, Henry Ford revolutionized the automobile industry and manufacturing itself. With the development of the mass-produced Model T, he became the first to make cars available to the general public. Ford was, however, unable to sustain the virtue of rationality throughout his career. In the 1920s, he squandered his company's commanding position in the auto industry to Chevrolet by refusing to expand its product lines. During the Great Depression, he abandoned reason as a management precept and used fear to rule his assembly workers. Later, Ford slipped into increasingly irrational behavior and, in 1945, had to be forced out of the company he created.

RESPONSIBILITIES OF RATIONALITY

In his book *Objectivism*, Rand's heir Leonard Peikoff described the virtue of rationality as a "primary obligation of man."[5] The word "obligation" is well chosen; rationality brings with it responsibilities. Responsible rationality requires that we set our goals based on reality, make decisions and take action based on reason, and accept the consequences of those actions.

Rand based responsible rationality on the law of cause and effect. We cause actions to occur and we are responsible for the effects that result. Any attempt to either act without being accountable for the results or to attain results without acting sidesteps responsibility. Both are irrational behaviors and, to Objectivists, evil acts.

The October 31, 2000, crash of Singapore Air's Flight SQ006 is an increasingly rare example of a corporate leader practicing responsible rationality. The flight departed during a typhoon that severely hampered the visibility of the three pilots aboard the plane and the airport's control tower. Taxiing down the wrong runway, the jet collided with concrete barricades. Tragically, eighty-two passengers were killed. A complete investigation of the accident will take years, but as soon as it was established that pilot error played a major role in the crash, the company accepted the facts of the case. Three days after the accident and before investigators made any public findings, Singapore Air CEO Cheong Choong Kong assumed responsibility, apologized and offered the families of the victims $400,000 (five times the legal liability limit). He told the press, "They were our pilots, it was our aircraft, the aircraft should not have been on that runway... we accept full responsibility."[6]

The response of company leaders during Bridgestone/ Firestone's tire recall controversy stands in stark contrast to Singapore Air's actions. Even after defects in the company's tires were linked to more than 150 deaths, the company attempted to limit its responsibility for its products. It failed to respond to initial evidence of tire failure, withheld information from the investigation, and tried to evade responsibility by blaming its major customer, Ford Motor Company, for improper tire installation. In October 2000, the company's Japanese parent took matters into its own hands and replaced the subsidiary's CEO Masatoshi Ono. "The responsibility is ours," said new CEO John Lampe in his first statement to the press.[7]

Rationality's Supporting Virtues

Practicing rationality also means the recognition and acceptance of four supporting virtues: Independence, Integrity, Honesty, and Justice. These virtues are specific components of rationality and they offer greater insight into what it means to act rationally. Rand described them as follows: The virtue of independence requires that individuals depend first and foremost on their own minds and judgments. Integrity requires that individuals act in accordance with rational convictions. Honesty requires that individuals refuse to fake reality. Justice requires that people judge one another objectively and interact according to that judgment. These supporting virtues are explored in the next four chapters.

6

INDEPENDENCE

THE VIRTUE OF INDEPENDENCE is an inextricably interwoven component of the primary virtue of rationality. In order to live
rationally—that is, to make a lifelong, concerted effort to
think—an individual must be independent in thought and
in action.

Rand's heir and philosopher Leonard Peikoff rightly labels the phrase "independent thinking" a redundancy.[1] In the
logic of Objectivism the two virtues cannot be separated: by
definition, rationality is an impossibility if the thinker is
blindly dependent on other people's conclusions, and independence is an impossibility if the thinker refuses to exercise
his own mind.

In a world that is increasingly dominated by systems
thinking, complex networks, and interdependence, independence is often seen as an anachronistic quality. Somehow, ex-
perts suggest, individual independence is the result of a group
effort. The Internet, for instance, is pointed to as a creation of
the collective mind and collective action. In fact, as Ayn Rand

would tell you, the exact opposite is true. The Internet was created by a series of individual actions over which no group has total control. It is the sum of those individual actions that resulted in the worldwide electronic network.

"But the mind is an attribute of the individual. There is no such thing as a collective brain. There is no such thing as a collective thought," Rand has Howard Roark argue in his statement before the jury in *The Fountainhead*.[2] Independence is the quality and the virtue that makes individual thought possible.

The struggle for personal independence is a theme that echoes throughout Rand's fiction. It is also the major theme of the science fiction novelette *Anthem*, which the author first conceived while still living in Russia and wrote late in the summer of 1937 during a respite in her labors on *The Fountainhead*.

In *Anthem*, Rand created a world in which individual independence is so alien a concept that words such as "me" and "mine" are not even a part of the language. Independence has not only ceased to exist, it has, in fact, been purposely eradicated and it is illegal. Using the word "I" is a sacrilege that is punishable by death.

Most of *Anthem* is set sometime in the future in an unnamed city, which is surrounded by the "Uncharted Forest." Governed by councils, life in the City is primitive and dreary at best. Electricity and the modern conveniences that contemporary readers take for granted have disappeared. To live to the age of forty-five is a rare occurrence. There are no families; people live in gender-segregated dormitories and are organized into labor-based groups. Their careers are assigned and they work, sleep, and even mate by a strict schedule. These slave-citizens of the future are identified by telephone-like numbers, such as Union 5-3992 and Liberty 5-3000, instead of proper names.

But for all of the prohibitions, mental programming, and regimentation in *Anthem*'s city, society's rulers are unable to completely stifle independent thought. The hero of Rand's story is Equality 7-2521, who spends much of his life struggling to be a good citizen. He tries to suppress and deny his normal egoistic tendencies and intellect, accepting the daily monotony of his life, "dumbing" himself down, and trying to find satisfaction in his assigned career as a street sweeper. It is a struggle that he ultimately loses.

The book's main crisis is precipitated when Equality 7-2521 discovers an underground tunnel, the remains of a subway system. Instead of reporting his find, the independent street sweeper chooses instead to risk his life and turns the tunnel into primitive lab. He steals away for a few hours each evening and eventually rediscovers the principles and applications of electricity.

Equality 7-2521 believes that the magnitude of his discovery will prove so great that it will secure him forgiveness for his transgressions and an improved place in society. But when he delivers it to the "World Council of Scholars," his discovery and his independence are denounced. Shocked into action by this incomprehensible reaction, the young man escapes by leaping through a window and leaving the city behind, exiles himself to the Uncharted Forest. His ensuing journey and his discovery of a life of independence and free will provide the story's stirring final chapters.[3]

INDEPENDENCE DEFINED

Independence is the freedom from the influence, guidance, and control of others. To be independent is to be self-reliant. "It means," Rand explained in her speech titled "The Objectivist Ethics," "one's acceptance of the responsibility for forming one's own judgements and of living by the work of one's own mind…"[4]

Rand maintained that individual independence in thought and action is a prerequisite for all human progress in every field of endeavor. The willingness to stand alone and risk contradicting ideas that everyone else accepts as gospel truths is clearly a critical success factor in personal, organizational, and societal advancement.

Independence is also a prerequisite for the creation of personal wealth. No businessperson can prosper over the long-term by simply imitating another's products or services. Wealth is generated by the innovative creation of new products and services and by the improvement of existing products and services. Both innovation and improvement require independent thinking.

The proof is in the daily business headlines. Compare, for instance, the entrepreneurs who continue to prosper with those that sank with the deflation of the speculative bubble in Internet investment. The original thinkers and the best implementers, such as the founders and leaders of eBay, Yahoo!, and Amazon.com, are weathering the stormy conditions. On the other hand, the imitators, who chased the promise of riches with cobbled together business plans and other people's money, are declaring bankruptcy and closing their sites. They, and their investors, quickly learned that being online does not translate directly into success; success is produced by innovative and independent ideas.

The Randian emphasis on individual independence may seem to ignore the "greater good of society," but that is, of course, a phrase that would have immediately raised the hackles of the novelist-philosopher. First, she would have told you that there is no such entity as society; society is a collection of individuals. Second, she believed that individual achievements *are* the driving force behind the economic well-being of every other individual.

There are many economists and business thinkers who agree with Rand's perspective. George Gilder, for instance, disagrees with the Objectivist view of altruism and religion, but nonetheless calls Rand "one of the titans of the history of capitalism and freedom."[5] Gilder, who was himself a significant influence on the economic policies of the Reagan Era, wrote, "It is only individuals who can be original. Institutions shy away from unproven or unfashionable ideas. Therefore, they cannot afford to create new knowledge."[6] In his book *Wealth & Poverty*, he finds that individual brainpower, not money or institutional power, is the foundational element of capitalism and the impetus behind the rise of the national economies.

The Objectivist vision of the virtue of independence is often exaggerated and misconstrued. It does not, for example, require that individuals become totally self-sustaining by producing everything that they need to live, including their food, clothing, and other products, on their own. Instead, it requires that we act as fully responsible members of society and trade fair value for the goods and services we need.

Nor does the Objectivist view require that we isolate ourselves from the rest of the world in order to live independently. Instead, it means that we should be and are free to pursue rational values in our lives and careers. Rand simply said that we should not mindlessly accept societal or other externally imposed beliefs, and that people should think them through on their own and decide for themselves whether or not society's mores should be accepted.

Correspondingly, practicing the virtue of independence does not mean that people are required to reinvent the sum total of world knowledge in order to live their lives. Again, independence means that we should not blindly accept the ideas and concepts of others. Instead, it is our responsibility to evaluate them to the best of our ability and ensure that they are logical and rational before adopting them.

Finally, this Objectivist virtue does not mean that whatever each independent individual chooses to think and do is right and proper. Independence is not a free pass to irrationality or hedonism. Instead, independence must be practiced within the larger moral constraints and logical context of Objectivism. Independent conclusions are not right because they are reached independently, but because they are rational and conform to natural laws.

All of the conditions mentioned in the previous paragraphs are related to the two major components of Rand's definition of independence. The first is the intellectual component of the virtue. It is the responsibility and the right to rely on the conclusions of your own mind. The second component of independence is the physical manifestation of the virtue. It is the corresponding responsibility and right to act and benefit from those intellectual conclusions.

INDEPENDENCE OF MIND

"All great truths begin as blasphemies," wrote George Bernard Shaw, and that is exactly why the virtue of independence in thought is so important to a successful career. Independence is the personal attribute that enables an individual to break with tradition and to conceive products and services that are new and different.

The history of The Walt Disney Company provides a good example of importance and power of independent thinking. Walt Disney, as we have already seen, was an innovator and independent thinker, but after his death in 1966, the company's creative output slowed and its growth began to stagnate. After Walt's brother Roy died in 1972, the management of the company maintained the family values that made Disney famous, but it was unable to generate the independent creativity that had captivated audiences for half a century. By 1984, the company's annual earnings had been falling for several years and with the stock price heavily depressed, Disney was in imminent danger of being taken over and sold off piece by piece.

Instead, in September 1984, Roy Disney (Walt's nephew and the company's largest shareholder) successfully fought to replace the management team, and Michael Eisner and Frank Wells took control. Eisner's first order of business was to restore the creative and independent spirit of the company. For instance, at the end of his second week at Disney, Eisner met with the executives in charge of the company's real estate development operations. He started the meeting by swinging for the fences. "How about designing a hotel right here in Burbank shaped like Mickey Mouse?" he asked.[7] The idea galvanized everyone at the meeting. "Let's think independently and outside the box" was the message.

The results of Eisner's emphasis on new, independent thinking were beyond anyone's expectations. The Disney Company experienced its greatest period of growth during the years after he assumed control. Annual revenues of $1.3 billion in 1983 exploded to $23.4 billion in 1999. Stockholders enjoyed a 20 percent compound annual growth rate in earnings per share. The virtue of independence helped turn Disney into a high-growth stock.

Eisner's mouse-shaped hotel also illustrates an important codicil of Rand's admonition to think independently. His idea never made it as far as the drawing table; the Disney development pros at the meeting quickly turned up design barriers that would have proved impossible to overcome. Faced with these rational objections, the new CEO dropped the idea as quickly as he had proposed it. Independent thinking, he knew, requires what Leonard Peikoff calls a "primary orientation to reality."[8] No matter how independent the conception of an idea, it must still bow before reality.

Finally, Eisner's idea shows that independent thinking need not always be aimed at radical change. The hotel, in and of itself, would not have rescued the company. Instead, it was one of many relatively minor ideas that encouraged everyone at Disney to reorient their thinking and open their minds. All people can apply the virtue of independence to their thinking. At work, they can propose improvements to their own jobs and working methods. They can practice and build their ability think beyond the daily routine.

AYN RAND AND BUSINESS

INDEPENDENCE IN ACTION

As we saw in the last chapter on rationality, it is not enough to think about a virtue, we must act on those thoughts. Thought without corresponding action—that is, knowing what is right and not acting on that knowledge—is immoral to Ayn Rand and Objectivists. We must live by the work of our independent minds.

The act of living by the work of their own minds is a primary difference between the classes of people who Rand variously categorized as prime movers and secondhanders, creators and parasites, and money-makers and money-appropriators. It is obvious from her labels that Rand preferred the former in each pairing. Prime movers, creators, and moneymakers are all independent beings. They have the strength of character to act alone without the comforting support of tradition and popular opinion.

Some moneymakers seem to take an almost perverse enjoyment in their independent actions. "I just love it when people say I can't do something," said billionaire Ted Turner. "There is nothing that makes me feel better, because all my life people have said I wasn't going to make it."[9]

Turner, who could have easily been a character in one of Rand's novels, earned a huge fortune through independent action. His career as a business maverick began in the early 1960s when his father signed deals to break up his debt-ridden company, the largest billboard advertising firm in the South, and took his own life.

Ted Turner, however, was convinced that the business could be turned around, and he broke the deals that would have split up Turner Advertising. He not only saved the company, but expanded its operations into radio and then, in 1970, into television. In the 1970s, Turner pioneered cable television and founded CNN, the first twenty-four-hour news network. Over the next two decades, he assembled professional sports and film conglomerates. In 1995, he merged Turner Broadcasting with Time Warner in an $8 billion stock deal. Ted Turner personally benefited from the results of his independence to the tune of $2.3 billion worth of stock in the largest media company in the world.

Few of us will match Michael Eisner's corporate performance or Ted Turner's quirky entrepreneurship, but that doesn't mean we should think or act any less independently. Ayn Rand had only scorn for those who abrogated the responsibility and right of independence. "Independence is the recognition of the fact," declares John Galt in his famous speech, "...that the vilest form of self-abasement and self-destruction is the subordination of your mind to the mind of another, the acceptance of an authority over your brain, the acceptance of his assertions as facts, his say-so as truth, his edicts as middle-man between your consciousness and your existence."[10]

7

INTEGRITY

THE OBJECTIVIST VALUES ARE not a difficult set of goals in which to believe. Reason, purpose, and self-esteem are logical and uncontroversial on the surface. Translating the values into action, however, often brings those who subscribe to them into conflict with other philosophies and belief systems, as well as society at large. The virtue of integrity is the steadfast adherence to Objectivist values even in the face of opposition.

Integrity also implies the quality of wholeness. When a structure is solid and sound, it is said to have integrity. When individuals act on their beliefs and refuse to compromise them, they, too, are said to have integrity.

"My personal life," wrote Ayn Rand in a statement appended to *Atlas Shrugged*, "is a postscript to my novels; it consists of the sentence: '*And I mean it.*' I have always lived by the philosophy I present in my books—and it has worked for me, as it works for my characters."[1] Rand was not a perfect human being, but the preponderance of evidence about the author's life supports her statement. She was a person of integrity.

Integrity was an important theme in Rand's fiction from the beginning of her writing career. Long before she had articulated the philosophical basis for *Atlas Shrugged* and labeled it Objectivism, she was exploring the virtue of integrity.

In the decade between 1926 and 1936, her first in the United States, Rand had not yet articulated what values humans should pursue, but she had figured out that people must be true to whatever their values were in order to have any chance at happiness. They could not sacrifice their beliefs and their goals without destroying their lives. They had to have integrity, that is, they had to act on their convictions about what was right for them.

Integrity was the major theme of *The Husband I Bought*, a short story dating from 1926 that was the first that Rand wrote in English. Apparently, she never intended it for publication or, if she did, she planned to publish it under the pen name, Allen Raynor.[2]

The language of the story is stilted, giving the reader a good sense of Rand's struggle to learn to write in a new language and setting a starting mark that, when compared to a novel like *Atlas Shrugged*, shows exactly how hard the author worked to develop her craft. What is already clear in the 1926 story, however, is Rand's flair for drama and her interest in serious ideas.

The Husband I Bought is the story of a woman, Irene Wilmer, whose highest value is the happiness of the man she loves, Henry Stafford, and it reveals the intensity with which she pursues that goal. Irene marries Henry when he falls in love with her and freely gives up her fortune to save him from bankruptcy. She helps him rebuild a career and his place in society, and she lives to please him.

Then, Henry falls in love with another woman. He refuses the relationship out of duty to Irene, but she knows his feelings and engineers a scheme to make herself look like an adulterer. Irene gives Henry the excuse he needs to end their marriage and pursue his happiness with the other woman. In the Randian sense, Irene is a woman of the highest integrity, sacrificing everything for Henry, her highest value. The story also illustrates the destructive logic of altruism.

In 1933, Rand revisited the theme of integrity in her first significant success, the play that came to be known as *Night of January 16th*. The story revolves around the death of an unscrupulous and larger-than-life business tycoon, Bjorn Faulkner, whose financial empire had collapsed. Faulkner was killed in a fifty-story fall from the balcony of his mistress's penthouse apartment. He left a suicide note, but a witness had seen the mistress, Karen Andre, push a body, which is mutilated beyond recognition in the fall, over the railing. The play relates the story of Andre's murder trial, but Rand did not specify the verdict. Instead, she decided that each night, a jury drawn from the audience would decide the character's fate.

Rand constructed the play so that the evidence is evenly balanced, with neither murder nor suicide being conclusively proved. The jury's decision is finally reduced to a choice about Faulkner's integrity to his own sense of life. His wife and father-in-law claim that Andre killed this man who never lived by any rule but his own pleasure because he had repented his sins and was prepared to live the quiet life of a model citizen. Andre claims that Faulkner killed himself rather than give up the lifestyle he loved.

The audience-juries found Andre not guilty about two-thirds of the time in the play's New York run. Rand's own view of Faulkner's integrity was clear: "I am still asked, once in a while—and it always astonishes me—whether I intended Karen Andre to be found guilty or not guilty. I did not think that there could be any doubt about *my* verdict: of course, *she is not guilty.*"[3]

In each of the above stories, integrity is a driving force in the actions of Rand's characters, but the values that they uphold are not yet recognizably Objectivist. Rand began formulating those values in *The Fountainhead* and later in *Atlas Shrugged,* she would place the virtue of integrity in its proper context, showing exactly what principles it was meant to uphold and protect.

Integrity Defined

Integrity tends to be a vague concept in today's world, mainly because so few people seem to have firm convictions. In the United States, we talk about the country's Founding Fathers, men like George Washington, Thomas Jefferson, and Benjamin Franklin, as men of integrity. Today, it feels like an outdated concept. The integrity of candidates for public office is debated, but it does not appear to be a de facto requirement for winning.

Objectivists maintain that integrity is neither vague nor irrelevant. "It means," said Rand of the virtue, "that one must never sacrifice one's convictions to the opinions or wishes of others."[4] Without integrity, Objectivism, and any other philosophy, is simply an exercise in mental gymnastics.

Integrity is often mistaken for honesty, as in telling the truth. Integrity is related to honesty, but it is honesty in the connection between our beliefs and actions. In this sense, integrity grows from the Objectivist tenet that human beings are integrated creatures and that there is no separation between mind and body. If we believe one thing and act in contradiction to the belief, we violate that connection.

The virtue of integrity is a critical support of rationality. It ensures that the work of our brains is translated into action. In fact, people cannot achieve any of the Objectivist values—reason, purpose, or self-esteem—if they do not act in concert with their beliefs.

Conversely, irrational integrity is something of an oxymoron. The characters that we examined in Rand's early stories were people of integrity, but their integrity is not always clearly directed and, as a result, causes them harm. Integrity to an immoral and irrational philosophy (Objectivists often use Nazi Germany as an extreme example) is no virtue.

Finally, the virtue of integrity is not meant to imply that an individual's beliefs must remain fixed and unchanging forever. Rationality requires that people constantly improve and expand their knowledge, that learning be a continuous process. Integrity to reason requires that people adjust their philosophy and actions when confronted with hard evidence that their thinking is mistaken.

Rand made one such adjustment that was directly related to her thinking about the virtue of integrity. Integrity is a major theme in *The Fountainhead* and in the mid-1940s, as Rand attempted to articulate her philosophy for a nonfiction book, integrity played a central role.

In her journals for the new book, Rand wrote, "Integrity—the first, greatest, and noblest of all virtues—is a synonym for independence. Integrity is that quality in man which gives him the courage to hold his convictions against all influences, against the opinions and desires of other men; the courage to remain whole, unbroken, untouched, to remain true to himself."[5]

As you can see in this chapter, the second sentence of Rand's entry remained unchanged. But the place she assigned the virtue of integrity (and, in fact, the list of virtues themselves) would be dramatically altered by the time she wrote John Galt's speech for *Atlas Shrugged* in the mid-1950s. Rationality became Objectivism's prime virtue and integrity became a derivative of it. Rand's convictions had evolved, but the courage with which she supported them remained firm.

The Courage of Convictions

As we've seen, Objectivist integrity requires people to behave with the courage of their convictions. To fulfill that requirement one must not only have courage, but convictions, too. Courage without conviction is not a virtue; it is irrational machismo.

An excellent example of an individual who has embraced a set of fixed convictions and stuck by them is superinvestor Warren Buffett. If you had been astute enough to invest $10,000 with "The Oracle of Omaha" in 1956, it would have grown to around $250 million in 1999. Even if you had waited until Buffett took control of Berkshire Hathaway in 1965 to invest $10,000, by 1999, it would have grown to $50 million.

What has made Buffett so consistent a winner in a discipline that for many of us is more like a game of chance? The clarity of his philosophy about investing and the integrity with which he pursues it. Buffett is a value investor, a student of Benjamin Graham, who depends on a few sound principles to guide his actions. He never buys what he doesn't understand; he evaluates and buys the business, not the stock; he looks for solid profits and strong brands; and he invests for the long term. "Buy low, never sell" is a favorite tenet. The result, since 1965, has been an increase in the book value of Berkshire stock every year. It outperformed the S&P 500 in all except for four years.[6]

Given this record, it is ironic that Buffett should come under any pressure to compromise his investment philosophy, but that is exactly what happened in 1999. In that year, technology stocks, especially Internet-related issues, were the fad on Wall Street. A speculative mania developed that drove the prices of "new economy" companies ever upward and unduly depressed the solid traditional businesses that Buffett favors. Berkshire turned in a gain in book value of only half a percent for the year, underperforming the S&P by a record 20 percent. The stock fell almost 50 percent from $81,100 to a low of $40,800 per share.

The media and some Berkshire investors were quick to condemn Buffett's philosophy as the main culprit in the company's poor performance. Buffet, however, categorically refused to compromise his convictions. "Predicting the long-term economics of companies that operate in fast-changing industries is simply far beyond our perimeter,"

Buffett frankly admitted in his 1999 report to the company's shareholders. "If others claim predictive skill in those industries—and seem to have their claims validated by the behavior of the stock market—we neither envy nor emulate them. Instead, we just stick with what we understand. If we stray, we will have done so inadvertently, not because we got restless and substituted hope for rationality."[7]

In early 2000, the pressure on Buffett to compromise his investing integrity resolved itself when the Internet bubble burst. High-tech stocks lost trillions in value and many high-flying Internet companies declared bankruptcy. In the meantime, Berkshire Hathaway quickly recovered almost all of its value.

Integrity Is Action

Acting in accordance with one's values is a critical requirement of the virtue of integrity. Integrity is the consistent execution of an individual's convictions. In normal circumstances, integrity can be an easy virtue to practice. However, the real tests of individual integrity occur when faced with difficult choices, when integrity comes at a high cost.

It is rare to find a company that is consistent in acting on its principles in the best of times, let alone when integrity comes with unexpected costs. Johnson & Johnson (J&J) is a notable exception and it is often cited as the textbook example of integrity in action, mainly because of how its leadership responded to the Tylenol poisoning incidents in the 1980s.

Like many companies, J&J has a statement of corporate values, its credo, which was first formulated by then-president Robert Wood Johnson in 1944, the same year that it became a public company. The statement was first published as "An Industrial Credo" and its creator established it as the company's philosophy. It said that the company's customers, everyone who used J&J products, was its first responsibility. After Johnson's death in 1968, the credo lost some its luster, but it was revitalized and slightly revised in a corporate-wide campaign in the late 1970s that left the corporate commitment to its customers intact.

In late September 1982, the value of J&J's credo was put to the test. In Chicago, a still-unidentified person purchased bottles of the company's Tylenol Extra Strength pain reliever, laced about fifty of the capsules with lethal doses of potassium cyanide, and returned them to store shelves. Within twenty-four hours, seven people in the Chicago area died and the Tylenol capsules were identified as the murder weapon.

The company was faced with a dilemma of nightmarish proportions. Tylenol was the leading medication in its category and there were something on the order of 31 million bottles in homes, schools, hospitals, and on store shelves. It was quickly determined that the poisoning had taken place after the products had been shipped from the company, but the company managers decided to recall every bottle. The FBI and FDC opposed the idea on the grounds that it appeared to capitulate to terrorism, but J&J chairman James Burke responded, "Someone was using our brand as a vehicle for murder, and we had to remove the vehicle."[8] The recall uncovered two more poisoned bottles.

J&J replaced every recalled bottle of capsules with Tylenol in solid tablet form at their own expense. Further, it completely reengineered its packaging to make its capsules tamper-proof, adding more safety features than the government would specify in future laws. When it reintroduced the capsules, within two months of the murders, J&J also gave away coupons for 80 million free bottles of Tylenol in the new packaging. Consumers rewarded the company's integrity by remaining loyal to the brand. In months, Tylenol was again the best-selling product in its category.

Three years later, poisoned Tylenol capsules caused another death and in the investigation following the murder, poisoned product was found in an unopened bottle in which all of the tamper-proofing was still intact. No one could explain how the capsules were altered. Again, the company lived up to its credo. This time, Burke said, "We feel the company can no longer guarantee the safety of capsules."[9] The company discontinued the manufacturing and sale of over-the-counter capsule products worldwide.

As the leaders at Johnson & Johnson showed, people must be prepared to act in accordance with their beliefs. "Integrity," commands John Galt in *Atlas Shrugged*, "is the recognition of the fact that you cannot fake your own consciousness... that man is in indivisible entity, an integrated unit of two attributes: of matter and consciousness, and that he may permit no breach between body and mind, between action and thought, between his life and his convictions.[10]

8

HONESTY

THE PRACTICE OF RATIONALITY demands that we are honest in our thinking and with ourselves. It also demands that, as an ethical society, we are honest in our relations with other people. Rational thinking and living require the virtue of honesty.

"Man requires the greatest, the most ruthless honesty of observation and reasoning in order to reach as correct a conclusion as his rational capacity will permit," wrote Rand in her journals for her abandoned book titled *The Moral Basis of Individualism.* "A man willing to fool himself will collapse — and does — in his first attempt at thought."[1]

Honesty is a hallmark of Rand's fictional heroes. They are committed to living their lives without pretense or evasion. Sometimes they are forced into acts that are dishonest in society's eyes, but only as a defensive response to an irrational world — a circumstance that Objectivists accept as necessary. Conversely, all of Rand's villains are dishonest in the sense that they are, in one way or another and for one reason or another, attempting to evade reality.

Rand's most developed portrait of the consequences of ignoring the virtue of honesty in a business career can be found in the character of Peter Keating in *The Fountainhead*. Keating is the dishonest doppelganger of the book's hero, Howard Roark, and his approach to his career provides a dramatic counterpoint to Roark's approach.

From the novel's very beginning, Keating is evading the truth. Like Roark he is pursuing a degree in architecture, but, unlike the orange-haired hero, Keating has no feeling and little talent for his chosen field. He wanted to be an artist, but bowed to familial pressure. Although Keating led his class at school, his achievement is gained by giving others what they want, instead of through original thinking. His design assignments are completed only with Roark's help.

Taking a job with a prestigious New York City architectural firm, Keating quickly ascends the leadership ladder. But his advancement is gained by political maneuvering and driven by the manipulation of others. He eliminates his rivals while posing as their friend; he abandons his true love for the boss's daughter in order to get ahead. Again, Roark is surreptitiously assisting him with the inspiration for his designs; Keating is simply a glorified draftsman.

By his late thirties, Keating is an empty husk of a man who must produce a significant building to retain his position. And so, he turns to Roark for help once more. Admitting that he is a parasite, Keating sets the stage for his final scene by asking Roark to design the Cortland Homes housing project and allowing him (Keating) to take the credit for it. Roark agrees for his own purposes.

What is the result of Keating's dishonest, secondhand philosophy? Profit in the short-term, but abject failure in the long-term. Keating simply cannot sustain a career built on evasion and pretense, and by the end of *The Fountainhead*, he is forced to admit that fact to himself and then, publicly, at Roark's trial for the destruction of the housing project.

Keating is so thoroughly ruined that Rand does not bother to write a conclusion to his life story. The last time that readers of the novel hear of him is at the end of his court testimony. "When Keating left the stand," wrote Rand, "the audience had the odd impression that no change had occurred in the act of a man's exit; as if no person had walked out."[2] Such are the perils of dishonesty and of building a career and life based on the opinions of others.

HONESTY DEFINED

The word "honesty" is commonly used to describe the action of telling the truth in our dealings with other people, of not lying to them. In Objectivism, however, it has a broader meaning. The virtue of honesty, explained Rand, means "that one must never attempt to fake reality in any manner."[3]

While the typical enjoinder against lying warns of the harm the liar does to others, Rand turned that conclusion on its head and rejected dishonesty because it harms the liar. By lying or otherwise behaving dishonestly, she reasoned, we put ourselves in opposition to reality. Dishonest people end up trying to gain value by evading reality and convincing others that the pretend is real. In essence, the dishonest person is forced to gain value from other people, a course of action that Rand repeatedly showed to be disastrous.

Conrad Hilton, the founder of Hilton Hotels, took a similar view of dishonest behavior when he articulated his personal philosophy for living in his 1957 business biography, *Be Our Guest*. "Once you start it," he warned readers, "there's no place that deception can stop—and of course it has to start with self-deception, even if it's only the self-deception of believing we can get away with it. True, sometimes we are not 'discovered.' But all of modern psychology and psychiatry is based on the belief that our self-deceptions drive things into our subconscious where they make all kinds of trouble…" Rand would surely have agreed with Hilton's conclusion: "Be honest."[4]

So, Objectivists oppose dishonesty primarily for the impact it has on the individual who practices it. They define the virtue of honesty, like all of the virtues, as a selfish practice and, therefore, a legitimate one.

For all of the Objectivist emphasis on honesty in relation to reality, Rand's followers before that honesty among people is a virtue that depends on the context in which it will be applied. In a world that conforms to Objectivist values, honesty is the best policy. But the world that we live in is not always rational, and our obligation to behave honestly is not an absolute obligation.

"Lying is absolutely wrong—under certain circumstances," explained Leonard Peikoff. "It is wrong when a man does it in an attempt to obtain a value. But, to take a different kind of case, lying to protect one's values from criminals is not wrong."[5]

We have no obligation to be honest with those who are behaving dishonestly, nor do we have an obligation to be honest in our relations with an organization or government that is dishonest. The pirate hero of *Atlas Shrugged*, Ragnar Danneskjöld, provides Rand's most flamboyant illustration of the point.

Danneskjöld is one striker who is not content to let the world grind to a halt on its own. He commits criminal acts—sinking ships, destroying factories, and stealing gold—against the looters, who have been dishonestly seizing the property of the world's few productive minds. An odd version of Robin Hood, Danneskjöld is stealing gold and returning it to the rich producers from whom it was taken. He answers the looters with looting, the dishonest with dishonesty, and, in doing so, hastens their collapse.

In Rand's first published novel, *We the Living*, the heroine Kira Agrounova dishonestly initiates a love affair with a Soviet officer in order to obtain food and medicine to save the man she loves. In Randian terms, the girl's actions are justified by the evils of the political system that she is forced to live under. As we'll see in the next chapter and in an interesting contrast to Rand's robber pirate, Agrounova's dishonesty does not lead to any happy end.

The virtue of honesty can be applied to an individual's internal and external communication. First, Objectivists are internally honest in the relationship between their own minds and reality. They are intellectually honest, refusing to either deceive themselves or to be dishonest in their own thinking. Secondarily, Objectivists strive to be externally honest in their relationships with other people (except, as noted above, when honesty threatens the maintenance of more fundamental values).

Intellectual Honesty

Intellectual honesty is a devotion to understanding reality to the best of our ability and constantly, consistently, trying to improve on that knowledge. People who effectively practice this virtue are highly valued in the marketplace.

Listen to what David Ogilvy, founder of advertising powerhouse Ogilvy & Mather, wrote in his classic book, *Confessions of an Advertising Man:* "I admire people with first-class brains, because you cannot run a great advertising agency without brainy people. But brains are not enough unless they are combined with *intellectual honesty.*"[6] Like Rand, Ogilvy recognized that the only thinking that really matters is thinking that respects reality and does not attempt to subvert it.

The notion that we can somehow change reality by simply not believing in it or otherwise ignoring it can be a very dangerous practice in life and career. In fact, one can make a good case that the 1986 Challenger disaster, in which the space shuttle exploded and its crew of seven perished, was caused by a less-than-rigorous policy of intellectual honesty.

In the investigation after the disaster, its cause was pinpointed to a failure of the rubber O-ring seals that secured the sections of the Challenger's booster rockets. During the launch, on January 28, 1986, the seals failed and hot gas began escaping through the joints in the rockets. This caused a rupture in a fuel tank and the horrific explosion.

The postmortem also revealed that both Morton Thiokol, Inc., the company that built the Challenger's booster rockets, and NASA were aware that the O-rings represented a potentially fatal defect in the *Challenger*'s design. In previous missions, they had found that the O-rings often sustained damage and that the lower the weather temperature, the greater the damage. In 1985, Morton Thiokol created a team of engineers charged with solving the problem.

The temperature during that fatal launch was about twenty degrees lower than usual. Accordingly, during a prelaunch telephone conference between the Morton Thiokol engineers and NASA, the company's engineers strongly recommended that the mission be postponed. NASA appeared to accept the recommendation and asked that it be made in writing. But the written recommendation to scrub the mission was never submitted. Instead, the company's management tried to evade reality for business reasons and overrode their engineers' advice on the grounds that there was no firm data that the rings would fail. They approved the fatal launch, and the shuttle exploded after seventy-three seconds in the air.

Long after the explosion, the late Richard Feynman, a noted physicist who headed the accident investigation panel, provided a dramatic, and public, response to the fateful decision. In a simple experiment, he plunged an O-ring into a container of ice water. Pulling the ring out of the icy bath, Feynman let it fall to the table, where it shattered.[7]

Like rationality and its derivative virtues, for intellectual honesty to have any value, it must be translated into action. Morton Thiokol's engineers did not fulfill that requirement when they allowed their original judgment to be overturned. Sometimes an honest conviction that is not acted upon is no better than a dishonest one, particularly when the absence of honest action allows dishonesty to flourish.

"Intellectual honesty consists in taking ideas seriously," Rand reminded Objectivists in an article in her newsletter. "To take ideas seriously means that you intend to live by, to *practice,* any idea you accept as true."[8]

SOCIAL HONESTY

The Objectivist command to practice intellectual honesty implies that we should also behave honestly in our relations with one another. Social honesty, the commonly heard admonition to tell the truth, is a secondary component of the virtue of honesty.

Trying to build a career or a business based on a policy of dishonesty makes little sense. Such a strategy might yield a short-term profit, but no one can forge the long-term relationships with employees, suppliers, and customers needed for sustained success without practicing the virtue of honesty. Bernie Marcus, a cofounder and chairman of The Home Depot, illustrates that point with a story.

One day, a golfing partner told Marcus that he had gone to one of the home improvement chain's superstores prepared to spend several hundred dollars to replace a water faucet. Instead, a "stupid" employee had showed him how to fix it for $1.50, losing a large sale in the process. Marcus's golf buddy refused to tell him the employee's name "because you'll probably fire him."

"How about if I tell you I am probably going to give that person a raise?" replied Marcus. "Because that person did exactly what we want them to do. We are there to save money for consumers, not to sell them products they don't need. And you know what?" he continued. "You are not the smartest guy in the world, but if you ever had something go wrong with your household plumbing again, where would you go?" Right back to that honest employee, replied the golfer.[9]

Examples of dishonest behavior in business and career are, unfortunately, easily uncovered, and, as Objectivism predicts, the ultimate cost of such a policy is almost always higher than any short-term gain it generated. The tobacco industry is in the process of learning the real cost of its alleged attempt to suppress facts about the health consequences of smoking. Manufacturers of asbestos products learned the same hard financial lesson.

In the 1990s, "Chainsaw" Al Dunlap became famous for an aggressive brand of hardheaded, reality-based management that he called "mean business." Dunlap saved companies by ruthlessly cutting head count and restructuring operations. And that was why beleaguered Sunbeam Corporation hired him as chairman and CEO in June 1996.

This turnaround did not go as planned, however. Dunlap appeared to have worked his magic in 1997 when the company reported operating profits of $132 million. But, by 1998, unexpected losses had investors and the company's Board of Directors questioning Dunlap's results. In June 1998, as the company's losses continued to grow, Dunlap was fired.

After extensive audits, reality caught up with Sunbeam and it was discovered that the company's heralded 1997 results had been more a matter of accounting hocus-pocus than real earnings. In October 1998, auditors reported that Sunbeam "overstated its loss for 1996, overstated profits for 1997, and understated the loss for the first quarter of 1998." The $123 million operating profit of 1997 was reduced to $52 million and after special accounting charges, it was found that the company had actually recorded a loss of $6 million. The restated results prompted the Associated Press to report that "the company's remarkable turnaround last year under former chairman Dunlap never really happened."[10]

Sunbeam's phantom turnaround benefited the company in the short run, but when it was uncovered, the damage caused by the deception drove the company into bankruptcy. It also proved that Ayn Rand was right when her strike leader John Galt declared, "Honesty is the recognition of the fact that the unreal is unreal and can have no value, that neither love nor fame nor cash is a value if obtained by fraud..." [11]

JUSTICE

JUSTICE IS THE LAST of rationality's derivative virtues and it is the virtue that most directly extends the Objectivist ethics into the realm of interpersonal relationships. The virtue of justice explains how we should evaluate and treat one another. It also serves as one of the foundations upon which the political and economic systems espoused by Objectivism are built.

To Ayn Rand, justice was the objective judgment of other people and the act of treating them according to the dictates of those judgments. Like the other virtues, Objectivists believe justice is an individual's right *and* responsibility. Rand was vehemently opposed to either turning the other cheek or remaining neutral in the philosophical and the physical conflicts of life. "Judge, and be prepared to be judged," she commanded and warned in the same breath.[1]

Rand's unyielding stance is easily understandable in light of her history. She knew firsthand the consequences of the suspension of an individual's right to objective judgment and justice. As a teenager, she had seen what had occurred when the Communists gained control of her birth country. Her father's business and her family's personal assets were seized and "redistributed" as the government saw fit. Their personal freedoms, along with the freedom of all Russians, disappeared. The state now dictated the course of their lives.

Rand immigrated to the United States to escape the injustice of the new Russian system, but she did not leave behind the memory of life under the Communism regime. In her fiction, Rand repeatedly and vividly portrayed the logical results of injustice, of granting rewards without regard to merit (or, in the language of Objectivism, granting causes without effects). In *Atlas Shrugged*, an unjust economic and political system causes society itself to collapse. In *The Fountainhead*, individual justice is squelched under the pressure of spiritual collectivism.

Nowhere in the Randian oeuvre is the Objectivist version of an unjust society more dramatically illustrated than in the novelist-philosopher's first full-length novel and first published book, *We the Living*. Rand turned to her own life for the book's raw material. "For those readers who have expressed a personal curiosity about me," she wrote in her 1958 introduction to the revised edition of the novel, "I want to say that *We the Living* is as near to an autobiography as I will ever write."[2]

The plot of the novel was pure invention, but Rand drew the setting and the characters from life. *We the Living* is set in

Petrograd in the 1920s after the Red Army's victory. The novel opens with a virtual reenactment of Rand's own family history as the Agrounova family dejectedly arrives back home after years of self-imposed exile in the Crimea. They have returned mainly because they have nowhere else to go, and on their return they find only faded hints of what was once the prosperous city of St. Petersburg.

Life in Soviet Petrograd is drab at best. Unemployment is high, the population is poverty-stricken, and diseases such as cholera are sweeping through the city. Jobs, housing, education, and food are all doled out by party officials. Against this background, Rand drew three main characters, all related in a love triangle, all of above average intelligence and potential, and each of whom, in his or her own way, demonstrated the logical consequences of a society that has abandoned individual justice for collectivism.

Kira Agrounova, who Rand later said shared her own ideas, convictions, and values, is the story's heroine.[5] The young woman is a captive of the Soviet system and is forced to abandon her dream of becoming a construction engineer when the party purges the university of all students with bourgeois backgrounds (an event that Rand witnessed during her own schooling).

Kira is passionately in love with Leo Kovalensky, a confident, intelligent man, who initially refuses to bend to the communist system. Kira abandons her family to live with Leo, who soon contracts tuberculosis. To obtain the food and medicine Leo desperately needs, his lover initiates a sexual affair with Andrei Taganov. Andrei is a communist idealist, a hero of the Red Army, and a member of the secret police. He falls in love with Kira.

Rand used the deceptions and manipulations that these three characters must undertake and endure to illustrate the consequences of an unjust system. Each is eventually destroyed. Leo recovers from his physical illness, but Kira loses him nonetheless as he disintegrates morally, becoming a black marketer and a gigolo. Andrei destroys his own career to save Leo for Kira and kills himself. And Kira attempts to escape from Russia, as Rand herself did, but is shot by a border guard. On the final page of the novel, still unbowed, she dies and injustice reigns supreme in Russia.

Justice Defined

Philosopher Leonard Peikoff clearly defined the roots of the virtue of justice when he wrote, "Justice is fidelity to reality in the field of human assessment, both in regard to facts and values."[4] To Objectivists, the virtue encompasses the practice of rationally and objectively judging the actions and lives of people.

The proper purpose of justice is to ensure that individuals receive a reaction or reward that correctly corresponds to their actions. In a just philosophic system, the creator of an innovative new product would reap the rewards of his work in the marketplace. Conversely, his competitors could not wield force to acquire his formula and processes. (In *Atlas Shrugged*, Rand illustrates the point by having the exact opposite occur when Hank Rearden is blackmailed by the government into supplying the secret to making his new metal.) The virtue of justice means, she later explained, "that one must never seek or grant the unearned and undeserved, neither in matter nor in spirit . . ."[5]

Justice is the extension of Objectivist values to the judgment of people. It is "blind" to everything except those values; it ignores what Rand called accidents of birth. Objectivist justice does not suggest that everyone is equal, but it does apply equally to everyone. To grant respect or reward based on race or economic class or anything other than a rational moral code was evil, according to Rand.

The concept of judgment may sound harsh and unbending, and it can be, particularly for those people who try to subvert the Objectivist ethics. Rand and her followers were, and are still, criticized for the ruthlessness with which they dispatch dissenters both inside and outside of the movement. But the virtue of justice and its ensuing judgment is built upon Objectivism's view of man's nature as heroic. There is no original sin here and people are not inherently flawed. Therefore, Objectivists start the process of judgment from the positive position of human innocence.

On the surface, the practice of giving to others their just

due also may seem to contradict the Objectivist injunction to put oneself before others, but justice is selfish. When Objectivists recognize and reward people who are working from the same philosophical and ethical basis as them are, they are perpetuating their own beliefs and practices. They are raising the odds that when it is their turn to be judged that those judgments will also be based on a knowable, rational system of justice.

Justice is itself the basis for what Objectivists call the Trader Principle. "The symbol of all relationships among such men," Rand had John Galt proclaim in his radio speech, "the moral symbol of respect for human beings, is *the trader*. We, who live by values, not by loot, are traders both in matter and in spirit. A trader is a man who earns what he gets and does not give or take the undeserved."[6] The view of people as rational traders is, in turn, the basis for dealing properly with other people in business organizations and larger economic and political systems. (We'll take a closer look at this in part three when we examine management from the Randian perspective.)

With this basic understanding of the virtue of justice, we can start to examine how to apply it in our own lives and careers. There are two actionable components to justice. First, we need to determine the facts—the reality—relating to another person. And second, we need to judge those facts based on a consistent moral criteria and act on them.

Loyalty to the Facts

Justice, like all of Rand's virtues, is based on a knowable reality. Rand did not expect nor intend that people be subjectively judged by one another. Instead, and in keeping with the value and tenets of reason, justice must be based on factual reality. "How, then, is he to arrive at the right judgment?" Rand rhetorically asked of mankind. "By basing it exclusively on the factual evidence and by considering all the relevant evidence available."[7]

Factual evidence in judging people are the things we say and do, our beliefs and actions. Objectivists largely reject emotions and subconscious motivations as a basis for man's actions and for the purposes of justice because they believe the former are simply reflections of an individual's philosophical construct. Justice relies on an objective perception of a human being.

In business, individual justice based on facts is the proper basis for the assessment and advancement of our careers, but it is not always properly applied. "I'd say that one-third of our vice presidents still don't have a good gut feel for how to review performance and award raises," claimed T.J. Rodgers, the CEO and founder of Cypress Semiconductor, in his 1993 book on the company's management system.[8]

That conclusion is what led Rodgers to create a "focal review" process devoted to ensuring that all employees are justly paid for their individual performance. The Cypress review process forces managers to focus on the facts by using a software-based approach. Computerizing performance data helps managers organize and visualize the data regarding employee performance and compare an individual's performance with his colleagues. A secondary benefit is the creation of a physical record of the evidence on which raises are based.

Cypress judges its employees by organizing them into focal groups based on their job responsibilities. Then, it evaluates each one using a committee that includes a direct supervisor who has knowledge of that person's day-to-day performance, an internal customer who evaluates the individual's contribution to corporate goals, and a manager who is qualified to judge the quality of the employee's work. And, finally, the company uses a pairing technique to rank each member of the group against one another. The result, says Rodgers, is that the rewards of performance are objectively and justly distributed.

Unfortunately, not all managers and companies are as rigorous and as devoted to factual performance measures as T.J. Rodgers and Cypress. Cronyism and nepotism, as well as other forms of subjective and collective judgment, are commonly encountered in business. When they occur, the virtue of justice is subverted.

In a business, that is a dangerous event. "It all comes back to rewarding outstanding performers," explains Rodgers. "Great people expect to be rewarded. You can't reward great people unless you identify them fairly and accurately."[9]

Moral Judgment and Response

Once the facts regarding a person are established, the virtue of justice requires a judgment and a corresponding action. Like the facts themselves, the judgment and the corresponding action must also be objective—that is, they must follow the rational dictates of the Objectivist ethics.

T. J. Rodgers of Cypress Semiconductor is an outspoken advocate of objective justice. In 1996, he demonstrated the strength of his convictions and made a fine statement of the principle of justice after a company shareholder took Cypress to task for the fact that its Board of Directors did not include "women minorities" and "equality of sexes, races, and ethnic groups." The shareholder, in this case, the Sisters of St. Francis of Philadelphia and Sister Doris Gormley, its Director of Corporate Social Responsibility, withheld its proxy based on the lack of diversity among Cypress's directors.

Rodgers responded with Randian aplomb. In a long letter, which was also sent to each of the company's shareholders, he explained that the company needed directors with CEO experience, direct expertise in the semiconductor industry, and direct management experience as a customer in that industry. These criteria usually yielded fifty-plus-year-old males with advanced engineering degrees and a history in top management in several companies.

"Bluntly stated, a 'woman's view' on how to run our semi-

111

conductor company does not help us, unless that woman has an advanced technical degree and experience as a CEO," wrote Rodgers. "We would quickly embrace the opportunity to include any woman or minority person who could help us as a director, because we pursue talent—and we don't care in what package that talent comes."

Rodgers further accused Sister Gormley of suggesting that Cypress act immorally, arguing that settling for anything less than the best-qualified directors would harm the company's performance and do an injustice to its employees and its shareholders. "Choosing a Board of Directors based on race and gender is a lousy way to run a company. Cypress will never do it," declared the CEO. "Furthermore, we will never be pressured into it, because bowing to well-meaning, special-interest groups is an immoral way to run a company, given all the people it would hurt."[10]

Ayn Rand would likely have agreed with the justice of Rodgers's assessment of Sister Gormley's suggestion and his reaction to it. The Objectivist response to judgment is supposed to be tempered by the context in which an action occurs. To that end, Objectivists recognize different degrees of response. Rand explained this to philosopher John Hospers in a 1961 letter. "In personal relationships," she wrote, "the rewards might range from an approving smile to falling in love; the punishments range from a polite reproach (when the action involved is an error of knowledge) to a complete break (when the action is *proved* to be a willful, conscious, deliberate immorality)."[11]

No matter to what degree we act on our judgments of other people, Rand was clear that justice is an indispensable component of rationality. To give John Galt the final word: "Justice is the recognition of the fact that you cannot fake the character of men as you cannot fake the character of nature, that you must judge men as conscientiously as you judge inanimate objects, with the same respect for the truth, with the same incorruptible vision, by as pure and as *rational* a process of identification — that every man must be judged for what he *is* and treated accordingly . . ."[12]

Galt's declaration concludes our exploration of Rand's primary virtue of rationality and its four derivative virtues — independence, integrity, honesty, and justice — the behaviors through which Objectivists achieve the value of reason. In the next two chapters, we will turn to Rand's two final virtues: productiveness, which supports the value of purpose; and pride, which supports the value of self-esteem.

10

PRODUCTIVENESS

AYN RAND BELIEVED THAT for people to live worthwhile lives, they required a purpose. Purpose, she explained, provides the infrastructure for living, the framework that allows you to take charge of your life. For Objectivists, there is only one central purpose in life and that is productive work.

How each of us chooses to pursue the goal of productive work is our own choice. We may be businesspeople, journalists, academicians, or artists. Whatever we choose as a career, however, Objectivism demands that it applies "reason to the problem of survival" and yields material values.[1] It demands the virtue of productiveness.

Ayn Rand was not a prolific writer. In her lifetime, she published five works of fiction and six nonfiction books, which were usually comprised of reprinted excerpts from her fiction, speeches, and newsletter articles, as well as essays from other authors. Nevertheless, Rand's life is a testament to productiveness.

Rand was as rational, creative, and committed a worker as

any of her fictional heroes. In her early years, Rand worked exceptionally hard to establish her career as a writer, learning a new language and often working full-time at unrelated jobs to earn enough to support herself and her husband. Even at the peak of her writing career, Rand devoted all of the time and effort necessary to produce writing that lived up to her highest standards and full ability. The two years she spent on John Galt's sixty-page speech in *Atlas Shrugged* seems excessive on the surface, but in light of the content—an integrated philosophic system, it is a huge achievement.

Rand's most productive heroes echoed her own work ethic. Two, in particular, Dagny Taggart and Henry "Hank" Rearden, both major characters in *Atlas Shrugged*, are models for the virtue of productiveness. It is, in fact, their devotion to productive work and their reluctance to abandon the businesses they have created and managed that causes them to be among the very last to join John Galt's strikers.

"Dagny Taggart," writes University of Texas English professor Mimi Reisel Gladstein, "is probably the most admirable and successful heroine in American fiction."[2] In 1957, the year that *Atlas Shrugged* first appeared on America's bookshelves, Taggart was a woman well ahead of her time. Rand made the novel's female lead the vice president of operations and the de facto head of Taggart Transcontinental, the country's largest railroad. Taggart is productiveness incarnate and knows more about the day-to-day running and business strategy of the company than any other person, including her brother, James, who is the railroad's president but does not exhibit a glimmer of his sister's ability. She is intense, attractive, and unmarried, and nothing means more to her than her work.

Taggart spends almost the entire novel fighting to keep her railroad running in the face of a collapsing economy. It is a losing battle, but she wages it with an unparalleled degree of creativity and decisiveness. In her quest to save the railroad, Taggart accidentally sees Galt's Gulch, the community the strikers have built, and hears firsthand the philosophy that supports it, but that is not enough to convince her to abandon her life's work. Neither is falling in love with John Galt himself. It is a measure of her commitment to productive work that she does not give up the fight to save Taggart Transcontinental until the penultimate chapter of the book.

Hank Rearden does not hold out quite as long as Taggart against the strikers, but he is as much a paragon of productiveness as she. Rearden, in a fictional foreshadowing of the real-life story of Ken Iverson and Nucor (see chapter four), buys an abandoned steel plant and enters the moribund industry to widespread predictions of failure. Instead, by virtue of innovation and radically improved productivity, he builds the company into an industry leader.

Rearden is not content simply to make steel. He spends a full decade struggling to create a new miracle metal and, as the novel opens, he succeeds. Rearden Metal is twice the strength and half the weight of steel. It is also longer lasting and less expensive. Rearden has invented a product that has the power to revolutionize not only his industry, but every industry and product that uses metal.

As a result and in keeping with the upside-down world of *Atlas Shrugged*, Rearden is envied and roundly denounced. When attempts to suppress the fruit of his labor are defeated, the government seizes the formula for Rearden's metal and gives it to his competitors. Still, the entrepreneur works on. Finally, after the entire steel industry is brought under governmental control in a scheme in which Rearden's profits will be directly distributed to less-productive steelmakers, the industrialist comes to the belated realization that the only moral course of action is to not contribute to an irreversibly corrupt system. He joins the strikers.

Productiveness Defined

In Objectivism, productiveness is rationality put into action. It is the practice that turns the work of our minds into tangible goods and services. "The virtue of *Productiveness*," said Rand in her 1961 University of Wisconsin speech, "is the recognition of the fact that productive work is the process by which man's mind sustains his life, the process that sets man free of the necessity to adjust himself to his background, as all animals do, and gives him the power to adjust his background to himself."[3]

As Rand's statement implies, productiveness is much more than a contributing factor in personal success. At its root, production is a moral requirement in every human life and for human survival. Whether it is food, energy, or a myriad of other products, we obtain almost all of the necessities of life through some process of production. Even a century and half ago, when Thoreau retreated to Walden Pond, his return to nature was no rejection of productiveness. Instead, he attempted self-sufficiency, to take the production of his needs into his own hands.

As at Walden Pond, in an Objectivist world of free markets, if a person does not produce anything, he simply will not survive. Even in the mixed economies in today's nations, a nonproductive person may survive on welfare and charity, but he will surely not live well. Conversely, the more productive an individual can become, the better his living conditions will be.

In a specialized society, people are traders and they trade the products of their labor for the products and services of others. Money is the currency of trading and because it flows directly from the virtue of productiveness, from rationality put into action, Rand and the Objectivists view money, profit, and material wealth as profoundly moral.

"Until and unless you discover that money is the root of all good, you ask for your own destruction," declares copper king Francisco d'Anconia in a famous speech about the meaning of money in *Atlas Shrugged*.[4] In the language of cause and effect, productiveness and the other Objectivist virtues are the cause, and money is the effect. The rational pursuit of money, showed Rand, is accomplished by the same process that results in an improved quality of life. As it is morally right to pursue life, it is also morally right to pursue money.

Further, because of this chain of logic, Rand and the Objectivists preach the unrestricted value of production and wealth. They will not agree to limits on the achievement of either one. This is one reason why Objectivists disagree with environmentalists. In the face of mounting evidence to the contrary, Objectivists say that in reality, natural resources are available in infinite quantities and that human productiveness should not be restricted in the name of conservation. Man's creativity, they claim, will compensate for any shortages in nature.

Wealth itself is simply a byproduct of rationality. So, making more money means that we are making better use of our brains. "There is no human life that is 'safe enough,' 'long enough,' 'knowledgeable enough,' 'affluent enough,' or 'enjoyable enough'—not if man's life is the *standard* of value," writes Rand heir Leonard Peikoff.[5]

Finally, like all of the Objectivist virtues, productiveness is a selfish practice. But that does not mean that its benefits are somehow withheld from the rest of humankind. Objectivists are quick to point out that the progress of the human race has been and is wholly dependent on the gains generated by the productiveness of individuals.

The Means of Production

When Ayn Rand was a girl, she watched the Communists seize Russia's *means of production*—the factories, land, and capital that had generated the wealth of the bourgeoisie. Under the Marxist philosophy, the nationalization of the means of production was supposed to result in a more equitable society. What Russia's communists did not yet understand was that the human mind is the one critical means of production, what Rand called the motor of the world. And, as Rand would later show to great effect in *Atlas Shrugged*, a productive, rational mind cannot be collectivized.

Edwin Land, an inventor and the founder of Polaroid, sounded very Randian, when he said, "I think human beings in the mass are fun at square dances... At the same time... there is no such thing as *group* originality or *group* creativity or *group* perspicacity."[6]

Land, like Rand, knew that the foundation for the virtue of productiveness is the human mind. Our ability to think, to create, and to produce is all a function of the mind. Practicing the virtue of productiveness starts with using our minds to the fullest extent possible and developing the mind to its greatest potential.

Land pursued that potential with an intensity that few inventors have ever matched. By the time of his death in 1991, he had 535 patents registered in his name. He filed his first patent for an innovative plastic sheet polarizer in 1929, when he was a freshman at Harvard. Land was twenty years old at the time. Today, his polarizers are found in wide variety of applications, including liquid crystal displays, sunglasses, filters of all kinds, and scientific research equipment.

In the late 1930s and early 1940s, Land pioneered the field of 3-D movies and photography, and during World War II, he and his company created specialized visual equipment for the military. During the Cold War, he was instrumental in the development of the high altitude cameras used in the U-2 spy plane.

Land is best known for inventing instant photography. He produced the instant black-and-white camera, instant movie camera, and the famous SX-70, instant color camera. Instant photography was the technology that drove Polaroid's growth through the 1970s.

In 1980, Land stepped down as CEO of Polaroid after forty-three years and, in 1982, at age seventy-four, he resigned as chairman. Following his own precept that "anything worth doing is worth doing to excess," Land never stopped working. He devoted his last decade to research on human color vision and he founded, financed, and worked at the Rowland Institute of Science, a research organization that studies a wide range of subjects from artificial intelligence to protein dynamics.

"There's only nothingness and chaos out there until the human mind organizes it," said the prolific inventor in a *Life* magazine interview in 1963. "This is the most exciting part of being human. It is using our brains in the highest way. Otherwise we are just healthy animals."[7]

THE PROPER OUTPUT OF PRODUCTIVENESS

The virtue of productiveness requires that people use their minds for a practical purpose; that they create material values, the goods and services that, in turn, generate wealth. Objectivists do not value learning for its own sake. Instead, learning is meant to be directed at a goal and, more broadly, the achievement of the Randian values.

We can turn back to Edwin Land to see the principle in action. Land's greatest innovative efforts were all based on a practical impulse. The polarizers that resulted in the founding of the Polaroid Corporation began as a solution to the problem of headlight glare, a major cause of accidents in those years. The impetus for Land's invention of the ubiquitous instant camera of the mid-twentieth century was a question from his three-year-old daughter. Why, she asked, couldn't she see a photograph as soon as the image was taken?

Walt Disney's creativity had a similarly practical bent. He conceived the theme park industry during Sunday trips to a local amusement park with his two young daughters. While waiting for them to complete the rides, Disney critically appraised the tawdry surroundings, the surly employees, and the bored parents. Why not, wondered Disney, create a park where the whole family could enjoy themselves? The question became the basis for Disneyland and today's global theme park industry.

Ron Assaf can precisely date the founding of the billion-dollar, antitheft equipment manufacturer Sensormatic Electronics. On July 15, 1965, Assaf, then a grocery store manager in Akron, Ohio, was chasing a shoplifter down the city streets to retrieve two bottles of purloined wine. He lost the race, but began trying "to invent something to stop shoplifting."[8] That something turned out to be the first EAS (electronic article surveillance) system.

Each of three men described above provided fine examples of the Objectivist injunction to put the power of their minds to work for a practical purpose. They also illustrate the virtue's requirement of persistence.

Land envisioned the process of instant photography within an hour or two of his daughter's question. Later, after decades of work aimed perfecting the process, he humorously recalled, "Strangely, by the end of that walk, the solution to the problem had been pretty well formulated. I would say that everything had been, except those few details that took from 1943 to 1973."[9]

Disney spent years trying to convince his brother, Roy, who held the company's purse strings, to fund his vision of a theme park. Finally, Walt formed another company, Walt Disney Enterprises (which became the first incarnation of the now-famous Disney Imagineering division), financed it from his own pocket by selling his vacation home and borrowing against his life insurance, and started his park without Roy and the Walt Disney Company. Realizing that Walt would not be stopped, Roy capitulated and bought into his brother's unique vision.

Assaf, too, fought a hard battle to establish his new invention. After two years of development, no retailer would buy the first Sensormatic electronic security system. In 1968, he had to pay an Ohio retailer three hundred dollars per month to install the system. He installed eighteen additional system systems without charge before he finally got a paying customer. It was 1973 before the company recorded its first annual profit.

Land, Disney, and Assaf would not surrender the results of their productivity and they eventually achieved the success they had sought. "Productiveness is your acceptance of morality," stated John Galt in his radio speech, "your recognition of the fact… that work is the purpose of your life, and you must speed past any killer who assumes the right to stop you, that any value you might find outside your work, any other loyalty or love, can be only travelers you choose to share your journey and must be travelers going on their own power in the same direction."[10]

11

PRIDE

THE FINAL OBJECTIVIST VIRTUE is the virtue of pride. Pride is directly related to the Randian value of self-esteem. Self-esteem, which gives us confidence and trust in ourselves, is a product of pride. Pride is the work of creating the best, the most moral, version of ourselves that we can.

Pride, to Rand, has none of the negative characteristics commonly ascribed to it. In Objectivism, the virtue is completely free of arrogance and conceit. Instead, pride means the lifelong practice of the moral imperatives and behaviors of Objectivism. In this sense, it is the process of developing our spirit or soul.

Rand's grandest fictional heroes spring from the page. Architect Howard Roark and strike leader John Galt are men for whom the virtue of pride is already an integral part of their characters. They never seem to have any occasion to question their own intentions or actions. Their philosophical foundation is so soundly formed that it appears to have always existed inside of them and they act with the confidence that pride produces.

Conversely, the virtue of pride is completely absent in Rand's villains. The worst, such as Ellsworth Toohey, the archvillain of *The Fountainhead*, have the false pride of power-seekers. They seek to manipulate and control others by purposely subverting the Objectivist virtues. Some of Rand's villains, such as Peter Keating, discussed earlier in chapter seven, choose to live through the values of other people, and so, have neither pride nor self-esteem.

The development of pride is most evident in some of Rand's supporting characters. For these characters, the acceptance and practice of the Objectivist virtues and the achievement of pride is a struggle. They must work to reach the conclusions that seem so effortless to Roark and Galt.

In *Atlas Shrugged*, for example, Rand created a poignant minor character named Tony. Tony, fresh out of college, is sent by the government to ensure that the output of Hank Rearden's mills is sold only to the customers that it chooses. Nicknamed the "Wet Nurse," Tony is a product of a lifetime of collectivist education and, although he is intelligent, he has not questioned what he has been taught, nor has he had the life experience with which to judge it.

Two years of watching Rearden at work changes Tony's philosophy. Rand illustrates his change of heart with a scene in which Tony asks Rearden for a job: "I want to quit what I'm doing and go to work —in steelmaking, like I thought I'd started to, once. I want to earn my keep."[1] He is ready to take pride in his career, in his life.

In Tony's final scene, he is murdered while trying to warn Rearden about staged riots that the government has planned to ease its takeover of his mills. Rearden finds him fatally shot and crawling from a slag heap in order to complete his task. With his dying statement, Tony achieves his goal and feels the pride that comes from living according to his values. He dies moments later in Rearden's arms.

In *The Fountainhead*, the sculptor Steven Mallory makes a similar journey, in this case, to rediscover his lost pride. Mallory sculpts the human figure in heroic form; his esthetic sense of life (Rand's term) is Objectivist in nature. His work makes many people uncomfortable, perhaps because of the contrast between his vision of man and the reality that they live.

Mallory comes into the story when he loses a commission and shortly thereafter, seemingly without cause, tries to assassinate architectural critic Ellsworth Toohey. The sculptor drops from sight after the incident, but Howard Roark tracks him down because he likes Mallory's work and wants to commission him to create a sculpture for one of his buildings.

When Roark finds Mallory, the artist has given up the fight to maintain his integrity and the hope of finding anyone who shares his vision of mankind. He is drunken and living in a rundown rooming house. To earn a living, he sculpts plaster wall plaques that are sold in dime stores.

Mallory's discovery of a kindred spirit in Roark is the

start of his redemption and the recovery of the virtue of pride. He takes Roark's commission and returns to life.

PRIDE DEFINED

"The virtue of Pride can best be described by the term 'moral ambitiousness,'" explained Rand in her University of Wisconsin speech. "It means that one must earn the right to hold oneself as one's own highest value by achieving one's own moral perfection."[2]

In John Galt's speech in *Atlas Shrugged* and in much Objectivist nonfiction, pride is the last of the virtues to be discussed. That is because striving for the moral perfection of pride requires that we practice all of the other virtues. And that is why Rand had Galt identify pride as "the sum of all virtues."[3]

The Greek philosopher Aristotle, who was the only major influence on Rand's work that she acknowledged, saw the virtue of pride in the same light. Over three centuries before Christ, in *Nicomachean Ethics,* Aristotle said "Pride, then, seems to be a sort of crown of virtues; for it makes them greater, and it is not found without them. Therefore it is hard to be truly proud; for it is impossible without nobility and goodness of character."[4]

It may be hard to be righteously proud, but Rand's idea of moral perfection is meant to be obtainable. Moral perfection does not depend on money or material goods, social class, religious fervor, or philanthropy. Instead, it is achieved by the use of our minds, by how rationally we can think and act. As a result, pride is within the reach of every person.

Nor does Objectivism require that we transform ourselves into superhuman characters in order to reach perfection. Every individual has the ability to understand, accept, and practice the Objectivist virtues. Thus, every person has the capability to earn pride and achieve its reward, self-esteem.

In Objectivism, the opposite of pride is not humility. Rand saw humility as self-abasement, as the belief that we are not good. In her mind, that belief was a rejection of the primacy of the individual life. Instead, Rand identified guilt as the opposite of pride and maintained that people should never accept it—whether it was deserved or not.

Undeserved guilt is, of course, the antithesis of everything that Objectivists believe. The Randian vision of human beings rejects any version of original sin and maintains that people are born *tabula rasa* with clear, unencumbered minds. Further, Rand opposed any philosophy or system based on the implication that an individual is subordinate to any other entity.

Objectivists do admit, however, that there are instances where people deservedly earn guilt. These instances occur when people violate the values and virtues of Objectivism. For instance, Tony, the Wet Nurse, is guilty of unthinkingly supporting the looters in *Atlas Shrugged*.

The Randian response to earned guilt is to never accept it, to never live with it. Instead, guilt must be redeemed. People need to resolve character flaws that cause guilt and they need to make right the actions for which they are guilty. This work is the process of moral ambitiousness that results in the virtue of pride.

MORAL AMBITIOUSNESS

Ayn Rand believed that individuals are self-made beings, not only in the physical sense of wealth and property, but also in the spiritual sense of beliefs and character. Man, she said, "is a being of self-made soul."[5] Moral ambitiousness is the process by which individuals build their souls. It is the systematic formation of a person's character.

Objectivist philosopher Leonard Peikoff talks about three activities in the task of character building. First, it requires that we actively seek the objective truth in moral issues, that we make our decisions based on Objectivist virtues and using our rationality. Second, it means practicing the virtues, consciously repeating them until the behaviors become an integral part of our characters and actions. And finally, character building means never giving in to guilt, to identifying and resolving our errors, and never passively accepting our own flaws.[6]

American founding father Benjamin Franklin provides an

excellent illustration for the quality of moral ambitiousness. Franklin was a figure of worldwide renown during the eighteenth century. He was well known for his scientific achievements, for his political skills and role in the American Revolution, and for his tremendous success in business.

Franklin was not born to a life of privilege. His formal education ended at age ten. Like most working class boys of 1716, he became an apprentice, first at his father's tallow shop and then, at age twelve, in his brother's printing shop. He broke with his brother before the apprenticeship was completed in 1723 and left his hometown of Boston for New York. Franklin was seventeen years old.

Franklin spent the next few years working and traveling, but soon tired of living an unaccomplished life. On his return from a stint in London, he began to lay out a plan for his future. Interestingly, it was less a plan of action than a plan of behavior. "I have never fixed a regular design as to life, by which means it has been a confused variety of different scenes," he wrote in his journal. "I am now entering upon a new one; let me therefore make some resolutions, and form some scheme of action, that henceforth I may live in all respects like a rational person."[7] Franklin had decided to build his character.

Biographer Carl Van Doren likened Franklin's effort to that of a scientist conducting an experiment. First, Franklin decided on a list of thirteen desirable virtues and reduced each to a short memorable description. Then, he ranked them in an order conducive to his adopting them. He recorded his virtues in a pocket-sized notebook, which he carried with him for decades afterward. Second, Franklin began to practice each virtue. He assigned each a week in an ordered rotation. During each week, he would concentrate on the corresponding virtue, thirteen weeks to work through the entire list and exactly four complete cycles each year. Third and finally, each day Franklin recorded and analyzed his lapses in an effort to understand his flaws and to correct them.

Franklin's concerted effort at character building appears to have paid off. In 1728, he started his own print shop in Philadelphia. The journeyman printer had no financial resources of his own, but used sweat equity to pay for a one-third share in the ownership of the shop. Within twenty years, Franklin had built that shop into the largest chain of print shops in the Americas, and he retired from an active business career as a wealthy man. And that achievement was only the first in a long, illustrious life.

THE REWARDS OF PRIDE

The virtue of Pride is like an upward spiral that feeds upon its own energy. The formation and use of the Objectivist virtues helps individuals live more accomplished lives. Higher levels of accomplishment build self-confidence and self-esteem. Self-confidence and self-esteem, in turn, encourage people to attempt ever more challenging values. Pride is a self-fulfilling prophecy.

Pride yields personality traits such as the courage to reach beyond accepted beliefs and the strength to attempt original and innovative projects. It gives people the assurance they need to stand up for their convictions, the assertiveness needed to accomplish their goals, and the ability to take pleasure in themselves and their achievements. Pride pays off in self-esteem.

The career of Jack Welch, the man that *Fortune* magazine named "Manager of the Century," is a good example of the benefits of pride. Welch shepherded General Electric's growth from a $25 billion company in 1983 to $129 billion in 2000. He presides over a company that employs more than 300,000 people.

When Welch took over as CEO of GE, he quickly earned the nickname Neutron Jack for his willingness to dispose of the business units and employees that he considered superfluous. In a controversial move, he insisted that GE rank first or second in the marketplace in every business it pursued. Units that did not measure up, more than 200 in the final count, were closed or sold.

By insisting that GE be the best in every one of its businesses, Welch captured the self-fulfilling prophecy of pride. It is at least a little easier for employees in GE's businesses to be self-assured, confident, and courageous. After all, they are already their industry's leaders and they set the benchmarks to which everyone else aspires.

Ayn Rand herself provides a fitting, final example of the power of pride. No matter what your final judgment is of her philosophy, writing, and the events of her life, it would be unjust to refuse to recognize the level of achievement Rand attained and the tremendous barriers that she overcame in her own life. Her pride in her own ability gave her the courage to pursue her dreams, to build a career based on novels of ideas, and perhaps, most improbably of all, create a new philosophic vision for living.

In *Atlas Shrugged*, John Galt declares, "Pride is the recognition of the fact that you are your own highest value and, like all of man's values, it has to be earned—that of any achievements open to you, the one that makes all of the others possible is the creation of your own character . . ."[8] Ayn Rand surely earned her pride.

3

Randian

Management

12

Winning Through Innovation

IF THERE IS ONE business book that we'd like to see on the packed shelves of bookstores, it is *The Objectivist Manager* by Ayn Rand. Unfortunately, Rand never wrote that book. But, in her fictional heroes, such as Howard Roark, Dagny Taggart, Hank Rearden, and John Galt, and in her nonfiction articles, she did offer insights into what it might have said. In this chapter, and the two that follow it, we will bring together those insights and explore the fundamental ideas that might have served as the basis for such a book.

Rand celebrated business innovators and entrepreneurs, and she argued that since the dawn of the Industrial Revolution, they have been the driving force behind all human progress. She maintained that the imagination and productivity of real-life prime movers are the engine of the world. She did not believe, however, that many of us deserved the designation of "prime mover."

"In today's conditions, it is impossible to guess their actual number," wrote Rand in a 1963 magazine article. "I once asked Alan Greenspan, president of Townsend-Greenspan & Company, economic consultants [now Chairman of the Federal Reserve], to venture an estimate of what percentage of men in our business world he would regard as authentic Money-Makers — as men of fully sovereign, independent judgment. He thought for a moment and answered, a little sadly: 'On Wall Street — about five percent; in industry — about fifteen.'"[1]

Rand created a guide to becoming a prime mover with her philosophy of Objectivism and that philosophy, of course, applies to the work of creating and running businesses. Like Objectivism itself, a book by Rand about business management would have surely been built upon the full and efficient use of the human mind. As we have already seen, for Rand, the value of reason, the virtue of rationality, and their application to the purpose of productive work were the cornerstones of a successful life and career. Here are some the implications of Rand's logic:

- It means that the productive application of brainpower, the creation of innovative products and services, is the proper foundation for business. Innovation — not customers, capital, or governmental controls — is the fuel of business success.
- It means that the most profitable and successful companies will be those that are able to innovate continuous-

ly. No one else can dominate markets over the long-term.

· Because the individual human mind is the source of all innovation, it means that companies that focus on the development, freedom, and independence of individual employees will be the most successful. Remember, there is no such thing as a collective mind.

· And, finally, it means that the ability to generate profit in the long-term is a natural by-product of brainpower. Whereas, the mindless pursuit of profit is a recipe for failure.

Let's take a closer look at these four statements and how they are supported by Rand's work and the evidence of existing companies.

THE FUEL OF BUSINESS SUCCESS

It often seems as though every business professor and consultant has his or her own theory for corporate success. At one time or another, customer focus, quality, speed-to-market, work teams, reengineering, and so forth have all been promoted as the key ingredient of a successful business. Ayn Rand offered a much simpler explanation.

" 'Economic growth' means the rise of an economy's productivity, due to the discovery of new knowledge, new products, new techniques, which means: due to the achievements of men's productive ability," Rand wrote in a 1962 column criticizing the policies of the Kennedy Administration.[2] For Rand, all economic growth, whether that of an individual, a company, or a country, was reducible to a single factor that must be obtained before all others: productive innovation.

Today, consumers are often identified as the key element of economic success, but Rand dispatched that notion a quarter of a century ago. Consumption presupposes production, she argued. A consumer is simply a producer with something to trade. Rand's reasoning may have verged on an exercise in semantics, but in fact, while customers may fuel markets, they don't create them.

"Over the years," said Polaroid founder Edwin Land, "I have learned that every significant invention has several characteristics. By definition it must be startling, unexpected, and must come to a world that is not prepared for it. If the world were prepared for it, it would not be much of an invention."[3] Customers did not ask for fax machines, cable television, or Internet service. Innovators created them and consumer demand followed.

Likewise, capital is often pegged as the key element of economic success, but money, as we will see in this chapter's last section, is a byproduct of innovation. In an industrial society, capital, explained Rand, represents a surplus of production. So, as with consumers, the concept of capital presupposes production.

It is also clear that while capital can fund operations and

WINNING THROUGH INNOVATION

enable a company to operate, it cannot generate corporate success. Iridium, the bankrupt satellite telephone network, provides an obvious example. It enjoyed billions of dollars in funding from a consortium of international corporations and the equity markets and it failed nevertheless.

George Gilder suggests that "wealth is a product less of money than of mind." He writes, "The only stable asset among the quakes and shadows is a disciplined mind. Matter melts, but mind and will can flash for a while ahead of the uncertain crowd, beam visions across the sky, and induce their incarnation in silicon and cement before the competition gathers."[4]

Finally, there are those who look to government to control the economy and to ensure corporate success. *Atlas Shrugged* was Rand's eloquent response to advocates of governmental intervention in the marketplace. In that book, government control guarantees that no company leads its industry, and finally, that no company succeeds at all. Everyone fails together.

The economies of countries such as the former Soviet Union and China support Rand's vision of politically controlled economies. Japan, which for a time boasted one of the most vibrant economies in the world, offers a striking example of the long-term results of a governed economy. In that country, the short-term advantages of artificially low interest rates, protected markets, and governmental support eventually gave way to a prolonged recession.

"A free market is a *continuous process* that cannot be held still, an upward process that demands the best (the most rational) of every man and rewards him accordingly," wrote Rand.[5] Innovators the kings of free markets.

INNOVATORS CREATE AND LEAD MARKETS

Innovative companies are those that create the best products and services at the best prices. By virtue of that work, they earn the leadership positions in their industries. In a capitalist economy, where the buyers are free to choose the best value available, no one else can dominate markets over the long-term.

At its most powerful level, commercial innovation creates new markets and industries. Henry Ford accomplished that with his company when he created the mass-produced automobile. The most successful companies are those that can apply brainpower to the achievement of these breakthroughs.

Continuous innovation is the ongoing creation of new products and services and Rand logically defined creative work as the arrangement, combination, or integration of already existing elements of nature. "It is an enormous and glorious power—and it is the only meaning of the concept 'creative,'" she wrote in 1973.[6]

Business creativity can come in different forms. It might be the pioneering of a new distribution channel, such as Dell's direct sales of computers. Or it can be a new business model, such as eBay's online auction service. Or it can be new products and services, such as Polaroid's instant cameras and Southwest's low frills, high fun airline. In any case, to prosper in the long-term, a company must be innovative.

Without the viable goods and services that result from innovative productivity, a company has nothing of value to sell and eventually no physical worth at all. This is a very basic lesson that was driven home in the fast rise and fall of the dotcom sector in 1999 and 2000. Investors bid the stocks of these companies into the stratosphere because they believed that the dotcom's innovative business models would yield tremendous growth, an unassailable advantage in the marketplace, and corresponding profits. When it became clear that only a very few of these companies had truly achieved the innovations they claimed, the value of the sector collapsed as quickly as it had risen.

Sometimes, a burst of creative energy can propel a company into a leadership position, but no matter how powerful the force of a single invention, a company cannot maintain that role without continued innovation. The recent decline of blue chip companies such as Xerox and Kodak provide proof of the need to pursue continuous innovation to succeed in the long-term. Both companies have been unable or unwilling to keep pace with changing digital technology and are in danger of being left behind for good.

Xerox copiers dominated the market for decades, but with the spread of electronic networks, the need for copying paper documents appears to be disappearing. Similarly, Kodak was

the preeminent name in photography for much of the twentieth century, but now digital images are fast replacing film.
Neither the quality of Xerox copiers and Kodak film, their
financial resources, their customer service, nor their speed-
to-market can overcome the technological innovations that
are eliminating the need for their core products.

INNOVATION REQUIRES INDIVIDUAL ACHIEVEMENT

We have been talking about innovation as corporate trait,
but Rand would have quickly reminded us that a corporation itself cannot be creative. Creativity is a product of the
mind and there is no such thing as a corporate mind.

Instead, creativity is generated by the individuals em-
ployed within a company. "No work is ever done collectively,
by a majority decision," Rand has Howard Roark declare in
The Fountainhead. "Every creative job is achieved under the
guidance of a single individual thought."[7]

Cisco Systems has played a leading role in the development of the Internet and profited handsomely by acquiring
the innovative products it needed to stay on the leading edge
of its market. Along the way Cisco purchased scores of other
companies and CEO John Chambers is under no allusions
as to what his company is actually buying. "When we acquire a company," he says, "we aren't simply acquiring its

current products, we're acquiring the next generation of products through its people."[8]

3M (Minnesota Mining and Manufacturing Company) is another corporation known for its emphasis on innovation and its recognition of the fact that creativity is the product of individual employees. Founded in 1902, the company has a long record of product innovation. In 1999, it derived $15 billion in annual revenue from the sale of more than 50,000 different products in 200 countries.

3M started as a maker of sandpaper and abrasive wheels, and then in the 1920s invented Scotch-brand masking and cellophane tapes. In the 1940s, it created the first commercial magnetic recording tapes. In the past twenty years, the company has brought the ubiquitous Post-it note and the Scotch-Brite cleaning pad to market. The genesis of all of these products was the creative work of individual employees.

3M makes continuous innovation an integral part of its strategy by aiming to develop 30 percent of its revenues from products developed within the past four years. It fully recognizes the importance of individual creativity with its "15 percent rule," a guideline that asks its researchers to spend up to that percentage of their working time on their own, independently developed projects, and it quickly and willingly provides the funds needed to pursue that work.

The company also actively seeks to hire new employees who are capable of innovative thinking. 3M interviewed twenty-five of its best inventors in an effort to identify common personality traits that it could then search out in job candidates. It found that its most valuable employees shared six traits. They were creative thinkers, problem-solvers, results-oriented, hard workers, self-motivated, and resourceful.

Interestingly, those traits are very similar to the personality traits that Rand used to describe the Money-Maker. "The Money-Maker has an 'employer mentality,' even when he is only an office boy—which is why he does not remain an office boy for long," she wrote in 1963. Money-Makers are independent, creative thinkers who are committed to making the maximum effort. They do not need to be told what to do and they "make and take their own chances" based on their own judgment.[9]

The key to building a successful company is populating it with Money-Makers, those creative, independent people who are capable of innovation. The most valuable asset a company can accumulate is the brainpower of such employees.

INNOVATION PRODUCES PROFITS

"Wealth is the product of man's capacity to think," declares Francisco d'Anconia, the colorful copper king of *Atlas Shrugged*.[10] Likewise, profit is a product of a company's ability to convert employee brainpower into innovative products and services.

Once earned, profit becomes a resource for generating ever-greater levels of innovation. Rand believed that its proper use is to provide the funding needed to expand a company's activities.

The need to reinvest in innovation is especially clear in the pharmaceutical industry. Companies, such as Glaxo Wellcome and Merck, create new drugs, but as the patents that protect their discoveries expire, competitors rush similar products into the market.

Glaxo, for example, released Zantac, which became the world's best-selling antiulcer medicine, in 1981. In the late 1980s, it was contributing fifty percent of total revenues. Zantac's patents started expiring in 1994 and by 1999, contributed less than eight percent of total revenues. Accordingly, to succeed in the long-term, Glaxo reinvests more than half of its profits in the research and development of new drugs. In fact, since 1995, it has spent more than £1 billion annually in the pursuit of innovative new products and its goal, from 2000 onward, is to bring three significant new medications to market annually.[11]

Money, explained Rand, is an artificial convenience that was developed by traders to facilitate the exchange of products and services. If it is not backed by the value of those goods, it is worthless. Witness the historical photographs of men pushing wheelbarrows full of worthless currency in the attempt to buy a loaf of bread in periods of rampant inflation.

Companies that narrow their strategies to the pursuit of

money, that focus solely on this quarter's financial statement, have lost sight of the true source of money. They may obtain short-term success, but in the long-term, they are not *making* money. They are not creating the new products and services that produce wealth. Al Dunlap's short tenure at Sunbeam, which we explored in chapter eight, is an extreme example of what can happen when innovation takes a backseat to profit.

This is not to say that money or profit is an improper value. Rand called money the "root of all good."[12] Corporations and entrepreneurs are in the business of making money and it is, according to Rand, a moral pursuit. In free markets, if a company understands the nature of money and makes it by converting brainpower and labor into value, it can and should make a handsome profit.

13

MANAGING
PEOPLE
TO
THEIR
ULTIMATE
POTENTIAL

TRADITIONALLY, CORPORATE MANAGERS TENDED to have one of two views of the people who work for them. Some saw their relationship with employees in a paternalistic light. They assumed responsibility for the welfare and lives of their workers as a parent would a child. Others viewed employees as physical assets. They treated workers as raw materials to be purchased, used, and discarded. Neither view of people management made sense to Ayn Rand.

In Rand's Objectivist world, individuals control their own lives and each person is responsible for their own life. Further, no one has the power to use or abuse another person without his or her voluntary consent. The use of force in any relationship between people is immoral.

In an individualist philosophy, there is no real distinction between employers and employees. Rand saw all moral people as both producers and traders. Producers use their minds and bodies to create value and then, trade that value in the free market for the goods and services they require. The better individuals are at producing value, the more they can obtain in trade. This is what Objectivists call the Trader Principle.

"[The Objectivist ethics] holds that the *rational* interests of men do not clash—there is no conflict of interests among men who do not desire the unearned, who do not make sacrifices nor accept them, who deal with one another as *traders*, giving value for value," explained Rand in 1961. "The principle of *trade* is the only rational ethical principle for all human relationships, personal and social, private and public, spiritual and material."[1]

Rand's vision of people as producers and traders is based on her system of ethics and, in particular, the Objectivist virtue of justice. As we saw in chapter nine, practicing the virtue of justice means judging and dealing with people in terms of merit. Merit, in this case, being their adherence to the values and virtues of Objectivism—their rationality, their productiveness, and their self-esteem and the degree to which they achieve these goals.

Rand's ideas about the proper basis for relationships among people can be extended directly to the relationship between employers and employees. In doing so, Objectivism yields these basic statements:

· Employees are traders, not chattel. No one works for
  you; they work for themselves.
· Mutual respect and voluntary cooperation are the hall-
  marks of a successful employer-employee relationship.
  Coercion and force destroy productivity, innovation,
  and eventually, the party that resorts to them.
· The only proper basis for judging employees is objectively and on rational merit. Managers who hire, develop, advance, or compensate employees on any other
  basis are harming their businesses.

In the remainder of this chapter, we will examine how the
three points above are supported by both Rand and the experiences of successful companies.

Employees Are Traders

The essence of the relationship between employer and
employee is a trade, according to Ayn Rand. In its simplest
form, an employer agrees to trade money for an employee's
time and effort. Employment is a mutually accepted agreement, a voluntary trade, between a buyer of services and a
seller. Both parties are equally served.

Rand's concept of employment as a trade presaged today's
free-wheeling, free agent job market by decades. In the
1950s and 1960s, the paternalistic corporation was the com-

mon model. Employees often spent their entire career with one company and then, upon retirement, expected to collect a pension from their employer for the remainder of their lives. Job-hopping was looked upon with suspicion. Even into the 1970s, people were being warned that if their resumes showed too many employers, it lessened their value in the marketplace.

In contrast, in 1943, *The Fountainhead*'s hero, Howard Roark, was confounding the supporting cast of characters in the book by marching to his own beat. Roark takes jobs based on his own needs and negotiates his own terms. When his needs are filled, he leaves the job. If the terms of his employment are violated, he responds as necessary. To Roark, employment is a trade that must respect and satisfy the needs of both parties to remain in force.

In today's economy, Roark's view of the employment contract is much more common. Management thinkers, such as Charles Handy, urge people to think of their careers as portfolios of skills, to switch jobs often in order to build the value of their career portfolio, and to refuse to accept work that does not add to their overall experience.

Corporations, too, have largely abandoned their paternalistic role and the idea of employment as a permanent pact. First, it has become obvious that companies cannot offer lifelong employment. "The message of the nineties," said IBM's turnaround CEO Lou Gerstner, "is that no company in any region of the world can guarantee full employment. It's an empty promise."[2]

Second, the feeling of entitlement that results from a guaranteed job is antithetical to employee motivation and achievement. In Objectivist terms, the right to lifetime employment must be earned. To extend it to the undeserving is immoral and ultimately destructive.

Denmark's Oticon Holding, the world's oldest hearing aid manufacturer, acknowledged the fundamental nature of the relationship between employer and employee when it radically restructured its organization in the early 1990s. Then-president Lars Kolind reorganized the company on a project basis.

On August 18, 1991, Kolind blew up Oticon. He eliminated departments and job titles, reconfigured jobs around each individual employee's skills and needs, transformed the traditional warren of offices into large, open spaces, and outlawed paperwork in favor of informal dialogue.

The company established a free-market for jobs in which employees were allowed to choose their projects, working hours, vacation days, and training. Under this work system, project leaders compete for employees and employees compete to work on the most desirable projects. The voluntary nature of Oticon's new employment scheme may seem to lack control, but value is the driving force of the new system and employees that do not seek out and contribute to projects end up unemployed.

How did Oticon's performance fare under a market-driven job structure? In 1994, Kolind told *Industry Week* magazine that productivity and flexibility had clearly risen.[3] In more concrete terms, the new system helped double the annual revenues and triple the net profit of parent company William Demant Group between 1994 and 1999.

So, both employers and employees have been moving toward a more balanced, Randian vision of the employment contract. Employees, knowing that a single job does not make a full career, are thinking more like Howard Roark. They realize that the progress of their work lives is their own affair and that no matter who signs their paychecks, they are ultimately self-employed.

Employers, recognizing the reality of the job market, are also thinking of employment in project or portfolio-based terms. Like Oticon, more and more companies are hiring workers for fixed periods and projects. And many are treating their own workforce as a portfolio, continually moving full-time employees into new assignments governed by new contracts.

Cooperation vs. Coercion

A major tenet of Objectivism is its unequivocal rejection of the initiation of physical force. "Whatever may be open to disagreement," asserts John Galt in *Atlas Shrugged*, "there is one act of evil that may not, the act that no man may commit against others and no man may sanction and forgive. So long as men desire to live together, no man may *initiate* — do you hear me? no man may *start* — the use of physical force against others."[4]

Rand rejected the idea of physical force for good reason. Violence destroys rationality. It forces people to act at gunpoint. It negates the primacy of the individual, replaces value with arms, and undermines the rights of property.

The corporate use of physical force was not uncommon in the late eighteenth and nineteenth centuries in the United States. Illustrious entrepreneurs, such as Andrew Carnegie, John D. Rockefeller, and Henry Ford, sanctioned the use of violence to quell the demands their workers.

In 1892, a strike at Carnegie's Homestead steel mills resulted in a running gun battle between the workers and an army of Pinkerton detectives hired by the company's general manager, Henry Frick. Twelve people were killed. In 1914, striking workers and their families at Rockefeller-owned Colorado Fuel & Iron Corporation were attacked on Easter night. Nineteen men, women, and children were killed in what came to be known as the Ludlow Massacre. And, in 1937, Henry Ford's reputation as a friend of workers was forever lost when, in front of media, clergy, and local politicians, his in-house security force savagely beat four union organizers, including future UAW President Walter Reuther, outside Gate 4 of the River Rouge plant in Michigan.

Outright physical violence has largely disappeared as a management strategy, but less-overt forms of force are still in evidence. Some managers resort to verbal intimidation and threats to motivate employees. "Chainsaw" Al Dunlap was noted for his use of fear and verbal abuse in order to scare employees into improvement. His first meeting with the management team he inherited at Sunbeam stretched on for hours as Dunlap screamed at his subordinates and summarily fired one manager who had the nerve to stand up for himself.[5]

In chapter five, we examined the destruction of the train, *Comet*, and the death of its passengers in *Atlas Shrugged*. When the train derails, Kip Chalmers, a government official, threatens the jobs of everyone involved unless a new engine is found and journey resumed. His demand is met, but only by ignoring the reality of the situation and the safety of the passengers. So the *Comet*'s journey continues and Chalmers declares, "*Fear is the only practical means to deal with people.*"[6] It is his last statement before he and every other passenger dies.

Fear is so common an emotion at work that the late quality guru W. Edwards Deming saw fit to address it in his famous Fourteen Points. "Drive out fear," says Point Eight, "so that everyone may work effectively for the company."[7] As we have seen in the last chapter, innovation depends on the freedom to think and act. Fear, as Deming knew, impedes freedom.

Driving fear out of the workplace is a prerequisite for productive, innovative corporate performance. Lou Gerstner knew that when he took on the challenge of revitalizing a staid, sinking IBM. Aiming to build an entrepreneurial culture at the computer giant, Gerstner asked his managers to promote innovation and prudent risk taking. "[Entrepreneurial companies] encourage and protect their risk-takers, mavericks and china breakers," he explained.[8]

This is not to say that employers should be pushovers. Gertsner is a tough-minded manager who has little patience for ineptitude. So are many other successful CEOs — Bill Gates is famous for shooting down obviously flawed ideas with a snappy "That is the stupidest thing I've ever heard." Being open to new ideas and creative thinking does not require that a manager suspend reason and rational judgment.

Employees should be held accountable for their performance. But at the same time, employers cannot achieve long-term success if they do not establish a rational, objective atmosphere of trust, mutual respect, and freedom at work.

THE VIRTUES OF MERIT

Objectivist managers use the virtue of justice to govern their relationships with employees. They act toward and react to workers based on their rational, objective merit. In Randian terms, they never grant the unearned and never withhold the earned.

Hiring and compensating employees on any other basis

than merit may sound ludicrous, but it is a standard occurrence in the business world. In an effort to promote equality and redress past injustices, the government imposes legal restrictions on the hiring practices of companies. Compensation practices are similarly proscribed. The current corporate infatuation with creating a diverse workforce is a similar situation. Rand would never have agreed with any of these artificial restrictions on a free job market.

For the same reasons, Rand opposed the labor unions that dominated heavy industry in the mid- and late twentieth century. She agreed with the principles behind the founding and rise of trade unions. As long as they applied their efforts to the defense of a free market in employment and wages, Rand supported their right to organize and bargain collectively. When, however, the power of the unions grew and they endorsed governmental controls on wages, forced compensation beyond what the market would bear, abandoned merit for seniority, and restricted the rights of nonunion workers, Rand criticized them for their rejection of laissez-faire capitalism.

In Objectivism, brainpower and ability are the only values worthy of consideration in the appraisal of people. "Anyone who has ever been an employer or an employee, or has observed men working, or has done an honest day's work himself," wrote Rand, "knows the crucial role of ability, of intelligence, of a focused, competent mind—in any and all lines of work, from the lowest to the highest."[9]

Successful companies hire the best—the most able and smartest—employees that they can find and afford. Given the compensation programs that CEO T.J. Rodgers has implemented at Cypress Semiconductor (see chapter nine), it should come as no surprise that the company puts equal thought into its hiring decisions.

When Rodgers wrote the book on his company in 1993, only eighteen people, all vice presidents and above, at Cyprus were authorized to make job offers. But every manager is responsible for locating candidates worth hiring. Rodgers thinks that working managers themselves are best qualified to scout out and evaluate a potential employee.

Once a candidate is identified, a rigorous interviewing process begins. The first series of interviews concentrate on technical ability, work ethic, and values. Then, an aggressive group interview is used to test a candidate's responses under pressure. Finally, the company conducts thorough reference checks. All interviewers generate written reports that, along with references and test materials, are turned into what Rodgers calls "a hiring book."[10]

Microsoft is another company noted for its "interview loop," an intense hiring process, and its emphasis on a candidate's brainpower. ""I don't hire bozos," says Bill Gates, who tells his managers that they are better off if mediocre employees don't come to work at all.[11]

Objectivist managers hire based on merit and they pay on the same basis. Microsoft pays lower salaries than many of its competitors, but offers ownership stakes in the form of stock options. The company is famous for the number of employee millionaires it has created under that program. More than 2,000 software developers in the company's Class of 1989 became millionaires in just two years, according to the calculations of one Wall Street firm.[12]

Conversely, the idea of giving raises to unproductive employees is an irrational and immoral action to an Objectivist. At Cypress Semiconductor, where all employees are ranked, the size of annual salary increases is determined by achievement. "We give no raises to about 3 percent of our employees every year, a sign that they are low performers," explains T.J. Rodgers. "This company would die if 3 percent of the products we shipped were defective."[13]

The virtue of justice is the governing principle of Randian people management. Employees and employers are traders, exchanging value for value. The relationship between management and worker must be voluntary and based on respect. And finally, objective merit is the standard on which all aspects of employee appraisal should be based.

14

LEADING WITH PURPOSE

PURPOSE IS AN IMPORTANT element of Objectivist philosophy. Ayn Rand believed that all individuals must strive to attain a purpose, a vision of what they hope to become and achieve, even if it is as simple as basic survival. The central purpose of a successful and fulfilling life, however, must involve productive work. Corporations are created by and composed of individuals. So to be successful they, too, must have a vision to work toward and a purpose that revolves around productive work.

Managers are responsible for the formulation of the corporate purpose and the direction of the effort to achieve it. Rand acknowledged that fact in a 1965 article in which she defined the work of management as "the organization and integration of human effort into purposeful, large-scale, long-range activities."[1]

In the decades since, management theory has echoed Rand's

emphasis on purpose by placing ever-greater importance on its role in business. Studies of consistently successful companies have shown that corporate purpose, usually described in terms such as vision and mission, is a critical factor in the performance and longevity of corporations.

Without purpose companies, like people, are rudderless. Or perhaps they can steer, but in what direction and toward what end? Companies without purpose end up chasing markets and customers. To give a recent example: When the B2C (business to consumer) segment of the Internet industry became unpopular in the investment markets in 1999, companies without purpose tried to avoid the coming reckoning by simply declaring themselves B2B (business to business) companies. Of course, these companies, without compelling purposes or profits, were eventually forced to close their doors for good anyway.

Purpose has become accepted as a critical element in a successful business for the same reasons that Rand assigned it as one of the three foundational values of Objectivism:

- Purpose produces focus. Clarity of purpose gives managers the ability to choose and control the direction of their companies. It also provides the vision needed to create markets and lead industries. A company without focus splinters its efforts.
- Purpose is long-term. It helps managers overcome the myopia of short-term thinking and offers an extended

perspective that can last for generations beyond the lives of the corporate founders. A company without purpose has no staying power.

· Purpose unifies the efforts of employees and creates common goals. It can create cohesion among employees scattered around the globe and help target the efforts of diverse individuals on a single goal. A company without purpose cannot muster the united potential of its workforce.

In the remainder of this chapter, we will examine these three attributes of purpose in light of Ayn Rand's thinking and the examples of existing companies.

Purpose Generates Focus

Creating and pursuing a purpose gives shape and direction to both individuals and corporations. "[A central purpose] establishes the hierarchy, the relative importance, of his values," explained Rand of the power of individual purpose, "it saves him from pointless inner conflicts, it permits him to enjoy life on a wide scale and to carry that enjoyment into any area open to his mind; whereas a man without a purpose is lost in chaos."[2] The same is true for companies.

In business, purpose enables focus. Focus gives managers the ability to concentrate a company's energy and resources on its core business and forget about everything else. It gives them the filters through which they can analyze and respond to the world in terms of their own goals.

Management thinker Al Ries compares focus to a laser: "When you focus a company you create a powerful, laserlike ability to dominate a market. That's what focusing is all about."[3] Purpose allows the establishment of focus.

Internet equipment maker Cisco Systems is a good example of the power of purpose. In March 2000, at the peak of the bull market, Cisco, which was only sixteen years old, became the most valuable company in the world with a market cap of $555.4 billion.

Cisco's founders, Leonard Bosack and Sandy Lerner, had a clear purpose in mind when they opened for business. They begin Cisco in the time-honored Silicon Valley garage to sell their new creation, the router, a device that allows digitized information to move between computer networks. As new technology developed, the company, now under the leadership of John Chambers, broadened its product line, but kept its purpose—to supply the equipment needed to create digital infrastructures. By 1999, it was a $12 billion dollar company generating more than $2 billion in profit and supplying almost 80 percent of the physical plumbing of the Internet.

Intel was another great proof of the power of purpose. Aiming to commercialize the newly discovered integrated circuit, the founders of the company along with Andy Grove pioneered the silicon-based memory chip and then invented the first CPU, the microprocessor chip that is the brain of the computer and every other "smart" product. Driven by Grove's intense focus, Intel dominated the market and became the brand to beat.

Interestingly, Intel may also provide a negative example of the power of purpose and focus. Recently, *Business Week* heralded the emergence of "The New Intel" with a cover story on the company's diversification. In it, Grove's successor, Craig Barrett, bemoans the company's focus on chips. He thinks the strong purpose established by Grove is stifling new business opportunities. Intel's chips, he says, "are a dream business, with wonderful margins and a wonderful market position. How could anything else compete here for resources and profitability?"[4]

The right question is: Why should anything else compete with this "dream" of a business? Barrett is moving into ecommerce, consumer electronics, Internet services, servers, and phones. At the same time, Intel's market share in its core business of microprocessors is falling as its competitors take control of newly developing niche markets and usurp its former role as the most aggressive innovator in the industry. If the rule of focus and Rand's concept of purpose hold true, the new CEO may end up squandering his inheritance.

The point of all this is that a successful business leader brings an intense focus that the company's managers can understand, communicate, and pursue. The virtue of purpose is the source of that focus.

PURPOSE IS LONG-TERM

A successful corporation, like a successful person, must have the ability to sustain and pursue its purpose over the long-term. The very definition of purpose implies a long-term outlook; when Rand said that productive work was the central purpose of an Objectivist's life, she meant that it would extend throughout a lifetime.

In business terms, the ability to develop extended strategies is a key factor in corporate success. The onslaught of media attention can make it seem as though innovations and markets develop overnight, but in fact, they often take decades to come together and mature. Witness the Internet, which took a quarter of a century to reach critical mass, and the gasoline-powered automobile, which took three decades to reach mass production.

Rand declared that "the free market is ruled by those who are able to see and plan long-range—and the better the mind, the longer the range."[5] And she supported her logic with the fact that great innovations, such as the motor, the airplane, the power loom, and anesthesia, were all roundly denounced before they achieved widespread acceptance.[6]

Netherlands-based Royal Dutch/Shell Group (Shell) is known for the long-term view it takes in its strategic planning initiatives. The ability to think long-term is an important factor at Shell, which was founded on the ambitions of a forty-year-old Dutch tobacco plantation manager who found crude oil floating on the surface of streams in Sumatra in 1880.

Ninety percent of the more than $100 billion in revenues that Shell generates annually is generated by the production and refining of oil and natural gas, but the company is not depending on either source of energy as its mainstay through the next century. Shell's long term outlook for the future suggests that by 2050, expensive, pollution generating fossil fuels will be well on their way to being replaced by cheaper renewable forms of energy.

"Most people in the world still lack adequate access to convenient affordable energy," explained Shell chairman Mark Moody-Stuart. "There is demand everywhere for cleaner energy. Meeting those demands offer commercial opportunities."[7]

As a result of that thinking, in the late 1990s, the company placed new emphasis on renewable energy ventures. It formed a new core business simply called Renewables and is building a portfolio of companies that include operations in solar power, biomass (wood-based) power, and forestry. Shell plans to pursue its purpose as a major provider of the world's energy needs no matter what form that energy may take.

The car manufacturers with long-term vision are pursuing similar courses. Driven by advances in battery power, Toyota and Honda already have hybrid electric cars on the market and like Shell, they expect that the gasoline engine will be largely replaced within the next century. In early 2000, the less visionary American automakers announced that they would also develop and release electric cars in the next three to five years.

While we might not see a real-life version of John Galt's miraculous motor that Rand imagined in *Atlas Shrugged*, the long-term vision that is an integral part of managing with purpose is capable of generating tremendous advances. It is also an integral part of successful corporate management.

Purpose Unifies Effort

A corporate purpose enables managers to achieve another major component of Rand's definition of their work, the "integration of human effort." Purpose communicates the proper objectives of a company and unifies employees in the quest to achieve them.

If you examine the examples of successful companies, you almost invariably find that their employees understand the corporate purpose and are moving in sync to achieve it. They see the big picture and how they contribute to it. In turn, this gives their work meaning.

The strikers in *Atlas Shrugged* are united by a comprehensive understanding of their purpose. That understanding gives them the strength of will needed to abandon the material wealth and property they have created with their brainpower. And it gives a handful of determined men and women the power to stop the progress of the world.

An unusual carpet company named Interface, Inc., has also discovered the unifying power of purpose. CEO Ray Anderson founded the Atlanta-based company to make, market, and sell modular carpet tiles, a new product developed in the United Kingdom, in 1972. Anderson's company was a success and by the 1990s, it was generating a half-billion dollars in annual revenues.

The company hit a wall at that level and stayed there until 1994, when Anderson revitalized it with a new vision. Struck by the enormous amount of waste produced in his industry, Anderson dreamed of turning Interface into an environmentally sustainable operation, and eventually, a restorative one.

When Anderson described his vision to employees, they aggressively embraced it. They created waste reduction programs in the manufacturing processes that soon led to millions of dollars in annual savings. They created 100 percent recyclable carpeting products whose production requires significantly less energy. And then they reinvented the way commercial carpeting was marketed and sold by introducing a leasing option that cut the customer's total cost and allowed the company to recycle and resell its own products.

Some might dismiss Interface's vision as foolishly altruistic, but Anderson recognized from the very beginning that the petroleum-based raw materials used to make carpet and the waste produced in its manufacture represented a huge cost to the company. The first benefactor of Interface's new purpose was the company itself and within five years, the annual sales had doubled to more than $1 billion. By 1999, Interface was the world's largest producer of modular and contract commercial carpet.

Purpose is the unifying factor behind Interface's success. It provides a common vision for the company's workforce and is keeping them on track to achieve its goals. "A career requires the ability to sustain a purpose over a long period of time, through many separate steps, choices, decisions, adding up to a steady progression toward a goal," wrote Rand. "Purposeful people cannot rest by doing nothing; nor can they feel at home in the role of passive spectators."[8] The same holds true for corporate success.

CONCLUSION

Ayn Rand Reprised

Some eight hundred people attended Ayn Rand's funeral. On a cold March night in 1982, they filed past her open casket and numerous floral tributes, including a six-foot dollar sign. There were few notables among the mourners. *The New York Times* mentioned only the then-chairman of President Ford's Council of Economic Advisors Alan Greenspan, *Barron's* financial magazine publisher Robert Bleiberg, unidentified leaders of the Libertarian Party, and university professors.[1] The relative quiet of Rand's passing was a direct reflection of her final years.

Rand's death punctuated a decade of decline in her writing. *Atlas Shrugged*, published a quarter of a century earlier, was her last major book, and although she planned a new novel and a nonfiction exposition of Objectivism, she was unable to muster the energy and motivation needed to bring either project to fruition. In the early 1970s, she typically wrote only one article per month. After her bout with cancer in 1974, her productivity was further reduced. Her last books were collections of previously published articles and transcripts of speeches.

There was a similar decline in Rand's public appearances. With the dissolution of the Nathaniel Branden Institute in

1968, a slow withdrawal from public life began. Rand appeared on a few network talk shows in the 1970s, but seemed to be appreciated more for the shock value of her ideas than for any serious discussion of her philosophy. She also gave fewer and fewer speeches, declining most invitations.

Happily, the power of Rand's thinking is another matter altogether. Two decades after her death, Rand's philosophical tenets are stronger than ever. Objectivists still bemoan the state of the world and the evils of big government and altruism, but, in fact, events have proven out many of Rand's ideas and there has been a noticeable trend toward individualism and free market economies.

Politically and economically, collectivism has failed. The United States sacrificed 58,000 lives during the Vietnam War and was unable to stop the Communist takeover of the country. Yet, by the mid-1980s, Vietnam was nearing an economic collapse caused by its own programs. The tide was turned by a much-debated move toward a free market system. Vietnam, although still far from a capitalist nation, is moving in that direction of its own accord.[2]

In a real-life parallel to *Atlas Shrugged,* Communist Russia dissolved under what Rand would have quickly identified as the burden of its own philosophical flaws. Rand was right: a system based on need instead of merit is untenable. It stifles individual creativity and achievement and, instead, rewards corruption and cronyism. In 2000, an event that would have been unthinkable in Rand's lifetime occurred. The first Russian language editions of her books were published and Russian economic advisor Andrei Illarionov made headlines with his public support for Rand's ideas.[3]

In business, Rand's thinking now sounds downright mainstream. The driving force of the U.S. economy is the technology sector and it is resoundingly in favor of free markets and limited intervention. Aside from a handful of major competitors who stand to benefit handsomely from Microsoft's breakup, the government's antitrust prosecution of the software giant has been widely denounced. The recent election of George W. Bush has led to speculation that the government's case may ultimately be lost.

Aside from the overactive watchdogs of antitrust, governmental intervention in business has also lessened significantly in the past two decades. Major industries, such as telecommunications, utilities, and airlines, have been deregulated and myriad benefits in terms of increased competition, innovation, and, ultimately, reduced costs to consumers have resulted.

Rand's emphasis on brainpower has captured the corporate imagination. Innovation, human capital, and knowledge management have taken the lead as the critical success factors in business. The days of "check your brains at the door" are long gone. Today's employers want every bit of creativity their workforces can muster.

Gone also are the powerful unions of yesteryear. The influence of collectivized labor continues to shrink. Employees are "intrapreneurs" and "free agents." Employers are forced to compete for talent. Labor is an increasingly open market and the price of brainpower these days often includes equity stakes in the business itself.

An Obscured Legacy

All of the above events offer proof and support for Rand's ideas, but we do not mean to imply that Rand was the sole or even a major impetus for the above developments. It is, unfortunately, impossible to exactly trace Rand's influence. Even today, she remains an outsider, a rebel thinker, whose name is often associated with the image of an eccentric gadfly.

Some of the fault for that perception lies in the fact that Rand was an outsider. She was a woman in a world of ideas dominated by men, a foreigner in America, a screenwriter among textbook authors, and a philosopher with an undergraduate degree in a discipline dominated by doctorates. Some of the fault also lies in Rand's own behavior and personality. She could be curt, cutting, and harshly judgmental.

Unfortunately, in the twenty years since her death, some of the barriers to Rand's acceptance have not been much lowered. Ironically, her outsider status has been perpetuated by the actions of those who believe in her the most. The major schisms within Objectivism have never been mended and, in fact, continue to generate conflict and dissent among Rand's followers.

The most direct intellectual descendents of Rand are the Objectivists led by her heir, Leonard Peikoff. They literally claim ownership of the philosophy of Objectivism and are committed to its preservation as a complete and unchanging body of thought. Peikoff and his followers aggressively protect Rand and her legacy and attack any deviation from the Objectivist party line as defined by its founder and interpreted by her heir.

The major opposition to the official Objectivists does not, as you might suspect, came from altruists, socialists, or communists, but neo-Objectivists, a growing group that is composed of those Objectivists excommunicated at one time or another by Rand, Peikoff, and company. They advocate a sort of free-market Randism, believing that Objectivism is open to interpretation and improvement.

The neo-Objectivists and Objectivists are so busy battling each other that those who fundamentally disagree with Objectivism are rarely engaged. Further, the constant bickering over who has the right to speak about Rand and Objectivism results in fractured messages that generate so much internal criticism that their external credibility is severely compromised. Finally, outsiders, who are initially attracted to Objectivism through Rand's writings and pursue that interest, run headlong into the ongoing firefight and often end up wondering what happened to all that Objectivist rationality. Objectivism's internecine struggle is a major barrier to the widespread acceptance and understanding of Rand and her philosophy.

Rand for the Practical-Minded

As you may have already guessed, the least productive approach to understanding Ayn Rand and Objectivism is to get caught up in these controversies. The arguments between Rand's followers are never-ending and, for those who are interested in drawing their own conclusions about Objectivism, largely inconsequential.

It is also counterproductive to get overly caught up in the ongoing debate about Rand's personality and personal life. There is no requirement that you accept Rand as an infallible being or every one of her pronouncements as gospel or each of her novels as literary masterpieces in order to benefit from her ideas. Conversely, it is not necessary to completely reject Rand and her ideas if you decide that her actions were not always a perfect reflection of her ideals or find an error in her logic or a heavy-handed turn of phrase in her novels.

A HUMAN RAND

Ayn Rand did a superlative job of living up to her philosophy. The record of her achievements and the barriers she overcame in the pursuit of her goals provide ample proof of that fact. Rand, however, was not the perfect embodiment of the Objectivist ideal. She was capable of errors in judgment. One of those errors, her affair with Nathaniel Branden and its explosive conclusion, resulted in great pain and disillusionment for Rand and those associated with her.

By all accounts, Rand was a compelling thinker and speaker. Her mental acuity, confidence in her conclusions, and communication skills made her a natural leader. But, those traits also had a negative aspect that manifested itself in the destruction of many of her interpersonal relationships.

By the time of her death, Leonard Peikoff was the last member of the original Collective to have an ongoing, personal relationship with Rand. In a 1987 lecture, when Peikoff said, "I knew Ayn Rand longer than anyone now alive," he was acknowledging more than the natural attrition of time.[4] Many people knew Rand before Peikoff; she was forty-five years old when they first met. But none of those relationships survived. Peikoff himself incurred Rand's wrath over their thirty-year relationship. He described her anger as "an immediate, open storm of indignant protest," and he admits, "sometimes it was not justified."[5]

THE LIMITS OF OBJECTIVISM

Rand's Objectivism is a tremendous accomplishment. The very idea of creating a philosophy for living and promulgating the result of that effort is an audacious and ambitious dream. Rand not only had that vision but, against all odds, she went on to realize it. That is not to say, however, that every pronouncement that she ever made should be treated as gospel truth.

Rand did not hatch Objectivism as a fully realized philosophy. She developed it over a period of many years and, while doing so, she sometimes refined her earlier thinking and other times reached new conclusions that contradicted her previous thinking.

We have already seen an example of that process with Rand's development and revision of the Objectivist virtues between the conclusion of *The Fountainhead* and the publication of *Atlas Shrugged*. When she first described the virtues, rationality was not even included on the list. By the conclusion of her work on Galt's speech, it was the foundational virtue of Objectivism.

Further, Rand attempted to extend Objectivism's application into every aspect of human life, including music, writing, and sexuality. As a result, she often issued odd statements. For instance, Rand championed the music of Rachmaninoff, but found Bach immoral. She admired hard-boiled crime writer Mickey Spillane, but dismissed Thomas Wolfe as a hack. And she tried to reduce human sexuality to a purely rational and fully controllable process, a feat of logic that failed even in her own life.

A LITERARY JUDGMENT

Rand's fiction ranks high among the best-selling books of the past century. *The Fountainhead* and *Atlas Shrugged* are great reads, in which the author presented a melange of blockbuster movie script, heroic novel, and philosophy text. The result was popular, accessible novels that actually had something to say. Rand was not, however, a literary genius in the critical sense.

Most of Rand's early attempts at writing remained unpublished until after her death, for good reason. They were crude and stilted and Rand herself apparently never intended them for publication. She seems to have always had the imagination needed to create stories, but it took her years to develop a sufficient command of English to tell them well and even then, writing was not an easy or natural task for her. Rand spent over a decade working on each of her major novels and after *Atlas Shrugged*, never undertook the challenge again.

Rand also seems to have recognized the shortcomings of her early published works and in certain notable cases, extensively revised later editions. *Anthem*, for instance, was heavily edited before she allowed it to be republished in the United States in 1946.

These then are the ironies surrounding Ayn Rand. She was reason's greatest advocate, but did not always practice it. She created a practical philosophy that people can live by, but pushed it beyond its boundaries. She was a hugely successful writer, but not a great one. In each case, Rand had flaws, but in each, her abilities and achievements far outstripped them.

"Ladies and gentlemen," concluded Leonard Peikoff in a 1987 lecture, "in my judgment, Ayn Rand did live by her philosophy. Whatever her errors, she practiced what she preached, both epistemologically and morally. As a result, she did achieve in her life that which she set out to achieve; she achieved it intellectually, artistically, emotionally."[6]

We believe that Peikoff's judgment stands the test of objectivity. Rand's imperfections do not eclipse her achievements. More important, her philosophy of Objectivism, with its vision of a benevolent universe, the supremacy of the individual, and the values of reason, purpose, and self-esteem, offers a practical, moral course on which to guide your life and career. That is why Ayn Rand matters.

BIBLIOGRAPHY

Reading Rand

This bibliography of Rand's own work and books written about her life and philosophy is not intended to be a comprehensive list. Instead, it offers a select list of those books that we found to be the most important and accessible reading in their least expensive, most readily available editions. For those in a hurry, there are three must-reads on the list: Rand's *Atlas Shrugged* and *The Fountainhead*, and Leonard Peikoff's *Objectivism: The Philosophy of Ayn Rand*.

AYN RAND'S FICTION

Anthem: 50th Anniversary Edition (Signet, 1995). A science fiction novella about individualism lost and found, first published in 1938. This edition includes a facsimile of the original English edition with Rand's handwritten editing.

Atlas Shrugged: 35th Anniversary Edition (Signet, 1992). The story of the strike to stop the motor of the world. Rand's first complete statement of Objectivism and most important book, first published in 1957.

The Early Ayn Rand: A Selection from Her Unpublished Fiction (Signet, 1986) edited by Leonard Peikoff. Short stories, a movie synopsis, a stage play, and unpublished scenes for *We the Living* and *The Fountainhead* dating from the 1920s and 1930s.

The Fountainhead: 50th Anniversary Edition (Signet, 1993). The story of Howard Roark and his struggles in a collectivist world. Rand's best-written novel, first published in 1943.

Night of January 16th: The Final, Revised Edition (Plume, 1987). The play relating the Bjorn Faulkner murder trial in which the audience decides the verdict, first published in 1935.

We the Living: 60th Anniversary Edition (Signet, 1996). The story of Kira Agronova and her struggle to be independent in Soviet Russia. Rand's first and most autobiographical novel first published in 1936.

Ayn Rand's Nonfiction

The Ayn Rand Columns: Expanded Second Edition (Second Renaissance, 1998), edited by Peter Schwartz. Reprints from Rand's stint as columnist for the Los Angeles Times in 1962 and nine other previously uncollected selections.

The Ayn Rand Lexicon: Objectivism from A to Z (Meridian, 1988), edited by Harry Binswanger. A useful encyclopedia of and reference to all things Randian. Alphabetically organized by topic.

Capitalism: The Unknown Ideal (Signet, 1967). A collection of twenty-four previously published articles, mostly written by Rand, addressing capitalism as the only moral, rational political-economic system.

For the New Intellectual: Philosophy of Ayn Rand (Signet, 1961). Collects and reprints the philosophical speeches in Rand's fiction along with the original title essay, a fifty-page defense of reason over force and mysticism.

Introduction to Objectivist Epistemology, Expanded Second Edition (Meridian, 1990), edited by Harry Binswanger and Leonard Peikoff. Rand's most complete statement describing how man knows the world, including transcriptions of Q&A workshops. First published in book form in 1979.

Journals of Ayn Rand (Plume, 1999), edited by David Harriman. The bulk of Rand's working journals dating from 1927 to 1966.

The Letters of Ayn Rand (Plume, 1997), edited by Michael S. Berliner. A selected collection of the more than 2,000 letters in the Ayn Rand Archives.

BIBLIOGRAPHY

Philosophy: Who Needs It? (Signet, 1984). A selection of eighteen of Rand's philosophical essays dating, with one exception, from 1970 to 1974 and starting with her speech at West Point.

Return of the Primitive: The Anti-Industrial Revolution (Meridian, 1999), edited by Peter Schwartz. An expanded edition of *The New Left*, a collection of twelve of Rand's essays attacking the ideological liberalism of the 1960s. First published in 1971.

The Romantic Manifesto: A Philosophy of Literature, Revised Edition (Signet, 1975). A collection of eleven essays and one short story describing Rand's esthetics.

The Virtue of Selfishness (Signet, no date). Fourteen of Rand's essays dating from the early 1960s and describing the Objectivist ethics. It includes Rand's 1961 speech at the University of Wisconsin and five essays by Nathaniel Branden.

Voice of Reason: Essays in Objectivist Thought (Meridian, 1990), edited by Leonard Peikoff. Thirty-odd shorter pieces covering philosophy, culture and politics.

Why Businessmen Need Philosophy (ARI Press, 1999), edited by Richard Ralston. A selection of fifteen essays about Objectivism and business. Two are by Rand (including her 1963 article in *Cosmopolitan*); the rest by noted Objectivists.

BOOKS ABOUT RAND AND OBJECTIVISM

Branden, Barbara. *The Passion of Ayn Rand* (Anchor, 1987). The most detailed Rand biography written thus far. By a founding, and eventually exiled, member of the Collective.

Branden, Nathaniel. *My Years with Ayn Rand* (Jossey-Bass, 1999). A revised edition of the memoir by Rand's first intellectual heir and former lover.

Gladstein, Mimi R. *The New Ayn Rand Companion, Revised & Expanded Edition* (Greenwood Press, 1999). A fine sourcebook and bibliography to material by and about Ayn Rand.

BIBLIOGRAPHY

Gotthelf, Allan. *On Ayn Rand* (Wadsworth, 2000). A clear, concise introduction to Rand and Objectivism written by an Objectivist philosopher with the assistance of the Ayn Rand Institute.

Machan, Tibor. *Ayn Rand* (Peter Lang, 1999). An academic, critical
overview of Ayn Rand's philosophy by a "blackballed" student of
Objectivism.

Paxton, Michael. *Ayn Rand: A Sense of Life* (Gibbs-Smith, 1998). A lav-
ishly illustrated companion volume to the sanitized biographical documentary of the same name. Written with the official approval of
Rand's estate.

Peikoff, Leonard. *Objectivism: The Philosophy of Ayn Rand* (Meridian,
1993). The nonfiction bible of Objectivism written by Rand's intellectual heir. Required reading.

Sciabarra, Chris M. *Ayn Rand: The Russian Radical* (Penn State
University Press, 1995). An academic and well-researched look at the
influences on the development of Ayn Rand and her philosophy.

Torres, Louis and Kamhi, Michele Marder. *What Art Is: The Esthetic
Theory of Ayn Rand* (Open Court, 2000). Objectivism applied to art.

Walker, Jeff. *The Ayn Rand Cult* (Open Court, 1999). A critical look at
Ayn Rand and Objectivist Movement that deserves a read, if only for
its unremittingly negative interpretation of every facet of its topic.

Notes

Introduction

1. The quote appears in "Ayn Rand Goes Multimedia" in the September 11, 1995, issue of *Newsweek*, p. 8.

2. Rand's quote appears in Barbara Branden's *The Passion of Ayn Rand* (Anchor Books, 1986), p. 221.

Chapter 1

1. Rand's recollection of her meeting with DeMille appears in Barbara Branden's *The Passion of Ayn Rand* (Anchor Books, 1987), pp. 76–77.

2. A variant spelling is Alissa.

3. Rand's quote is from an interview with Tom Snyder on NBC's *Tomorrow* (No Free Lunch Distributors), July 2, 1979.

4. Rand's quote is from an interview with James Day on *Day at Night*, WNET, March 29, 1974.

5. Chris Matthew Sciabarra's *Ayn Rand: Russian Radical* (Penn State Press, 1995) offers a detailed look at Rand's educational experiences and the state of higher education in Petrograd in the 1920s.

6. B. Branden's *The Passion of Ayn Rand*, p. 68.

7. The *Playboy* Interview: "Ayn Rand", *Playboy*, March 1964, p. 35– 43.

8. The quote appears in *Journals of Ayn Rand* (Plume, 1999) edited by David Harriman, p. 48.

9. The story is available in *The Early Ayn Rand* (Signet, 1986).

10. Ayn Rand's introduction to *We the Living* (Signet, 1996), p. xv.

11. Ayn Rand's introduction to *Night of January 16th*, (Plume, 1987), p. 8.

12. *Journals of Ayn Rand* (Plume, 1999), p. 78.

Chapter Two

1. The quote appears in *Who is Ayn Rand?* (Random House, 1962), by Nathaniel and Barbara Branden, p. 209.

2. *My Years With Ayn Rand* (Jossey-Bass, 1999) by Nathaniel Branden, p. 43–44.

3. Neither Frank O'Connor nor Ayn Rand ever made any public statements about the affair. Both Nathaniel and Barbara Branden wrote books describing it in detail after Rand's death. The Brandens and the affair have largely been written out of all projects officially sanctioned by Rand and her estate.

4. NBI was founded as Nathaniel Branden Lectures and changed its name when it was incorporated.

5. *My Years with Ayn Rand* (Jossey-Bass, 1999) by Nathaniel Branden, p. 226–227.

6. Ibid., p. 351.

Chapter Three

1. William O'Neill's *With Charity Toward None* (Philosophical Library, 1971), p. 14.

2. The speech, "Philosophy: Who Needs It," was first published in *The Ayn Rand Letter*, Vol. III, No. 7, December 31, 1973, and Vol. III, No. 8, January 14, 1974.

3. *The American Heritage Dictionary of the English Language, Third Edition.*

4. *The Passion of Ayn Rand* (Anchor, 1987), p. 294.

5. For a more comprehensive, single-source description of Rand's Objectivism, the two best books are Leonard Peikoff's *Objectivism: The Philosophy of Ayn Rand* (Meridian, 1993), the most authoritative and detailed study yet written, and Allan Gotthelf's *On Ayn Rand* (Wadsworth, 2000), a fine, short overview.

CHAPTER FOUR

1. The quote and Rand's character sketch of Howard Roark appears in *Journals of Ayn Rand* (Plume, 1999), pp. 92–97.

2. Roark's speech starts on p. 677 of *The Fountainhead: 50th Anniversary Edition* (Signet, 1993). It is also reprinted in Rand's *For the New Intellectual* (Signet, 1961), p. 77.

3. *The Fountainhead* (Signet, 1993), p. 678.

4. Ayn Rand's *Atlas Shrugged: 35th Anniversary Edition* (Signet, 1992), p. 936.

5. Leonard Peikoff's *Objectivism: The Philosophy of Ayn Rand* (Meridian, 1993), p. 152.

6. Thaddeus Wawro's *Radicals & Visionaries* (Entrepreneur Press, 2000), p. 388.

7. "The *Playboy* Interview: Ayn Rand," *Playboy*, March 1964, pp. 35–43.

8. *Atlas Shrugged: 35th Anniversary Edition* (Signet, 1992), p. 936.

9. *Objectivism: The Philosophy of Ayn Rand* (Meridian, 1993), p. 307.

10. The quote appears in Michael Dell's *Direct from Dell* (HarperBusiness, 2000), p. 12.

11. See the entry dated September 29, 1943, in *Journals of Ayn Rand* (Plume, 1999), pp. 260–262.

12. See July 29, 1953, in *Journals of Ayn Rand* (Plume, 1999), pp. 648–649.

CHAPTER FIVE

1. Nathaniel and Barbara Branden's *Who is Ayn Rand?* (Random House, 1962), p. 44.

2. *Atlas Shrugged: 35th Anniversary Edition* (Signet, 1992), p. 619.

3. The speech is "The Objectivist Ethics," reprinted in Ayn Rand's *The Virtue of Selfishness* (Signet, 1964). The quote appears on p. 28.

4. Ibid, p. 22.

5. Leonard Peikoff's *Objectivism: The Philosophy of Ayn Rand* (Meridian, 1993), p. 221.

6. "Officials: Singapore Air pilot should have seen he was on wrong runway," Associated Press report, November 4, 2000.

7. "Lampe lays out agenda for Bridgestone/Firestone," Associated Press, October 12, 2000.

Chapter Six

1. See Peikoff's *Objectivism: The Philosophy of Ayn Rand* (Meridian, 1993), p. 255.

2. Ayn Rand's *The Fountainhead: 50th Anniversary Edition* (Signet, 1993), p. 679.

3. Ayn Rand's *Anthem: 50th Anniversary Edition* (Signet, 1995) includes the revised edition prepared by the author in 1946 and a facsimile of the original English edition with Rand's handwritten corrections.

4. The speech is reprinted in Ayn Rand's *The Virtue of Selfishness* (Signet, 1964). The quote appears on p. 28.

5. The phrase appears in George Gilder's preface to the revised edition of *Wealth & Poverty* (ICS Press, 1993), p. xxi.

6. Ibid., p. 72.

7. The quote appears in Michael Eisner's *Work in Progress* (Hyperion, 1999), p. 214.

8. See Peikoff's discussion of independence in *Objectivism: The Philosophy of Ayn Rand* (Meridian, 1993), pp. 250–259.

9. See Robert Goldberg and Gerald Jay Goldberg's article "Citizen Turner," in *Playboy*, June 1995, p. 160.

10. See Ayn Rand's *Atlas Shrugged: 35th Anniversary Edition* (Signet, 1992), p. 936.

Chapter Seven

1. The quote appears in Ayn Rand's *Atlas Shrugged: 35th Anniversary Edition* (Signet, 1992), p. 1075.

2. The story along with other early pieces and unpublished vignettes appear in the posthumous collection titled *The Early Ayn Rand* (Signet, 1986). Rand's heir Leonard Peikoff has been unjustly criticized for releasing this material, which gives Rand's readers a valuable look at her development as a writer.

3. The quote appears in Rand's 1968 introduction to *Night of January 16th* (Plume, 1987), p. 6.

4. The quote appears in Ayn Rand's *The Virtue of Selfishness* (Signet, 1964), p. 28.

5. Ayn Rand's quote appears in her journal dated September 29, 1943, in *Journals of Ayn Rand* (Plume, 1999), p. 260.

6. Warren Buffet's performance is recorded in detail in Andrew Kilpatrick's 1,179-page "Monster Millennium Edition" of *Of Permanent Value: The Story of Warren Buffett* (AKPE, 2000).

7. The quote appears in Warren Buffet's report to the shareholders in the *Berkshire Hathaway, Inc. 1999 Annual Report*. It is available online at www.berkshirehathaway.com.

8. The quote appears in Lawrence Foster's *Robert Wood Johnson: The Gentleman Rebel* (Lillian Press, 1999), p. 621. The author was a member of the team that responded to the Tylenol tragedy.

9. Ibid., p. 637.

10. See Ayn Rand's *Atlas Shrugged: 35th Anniversary Edition* (Signet, 1992), pp. 936–937.

Chapter Eight

1. Ayn Rand's quote appears in her journal dated September 29, 1943, in *Journals of Ayn Rand* (Plume, 1999), p. 261.

2. The quote appears in Ayn Rand's *The Fountainhead* (Signet, 1993), p. 677.

3. The quote appears in Ayn Rand's *The Virtue of Selfishness* (Signet, 1964), p. 28.

4. Conrad Hilton's quote appears in *The Little Book of Business Wisdom* (Wiley, 2001) edited by Peter Krass, p. 212.

5. See Leonard Peikoff's *Objectivism: The Philosophy of Ayn Rand* (Meridian, 1993), p. 275.

6. David Ogilvy's quote appears in *The Little Book of Business Wisdom* (Wiley, 2001), p. 50.

7. The details of Challenger disaster are recorded in Malcolm McConnell's *Challenger: A Major Malfunction* (Doubleday, 1987) and Richard Lewis's *Challenger: The Final Voyage* (Columbia University Press, 1988).

8. The quote appears in Ayn Rand's article titled "Philosophical Detection" in the January 28, 1974, issue of *The Ayn Rand Letter*. The newsletter is collected in *The Ayn Rand Letter, Volumes 1–4, 1971–1976* (Second Renaissance Books).

9. The incident is related in Bernie Marcus and Arthur Blank's *Built from Scratch: How a Couple of Regular Guys Grew The Home Depot from Nothing to $30 Billion* (Times Business, 1999), pp. 104–105.

10. See "Audit: 'Chainsaw' Al turnaround a myth" in the October 21, 1998, issue of *The Seattle Times*.

11. See Ayn Rand's *Atlas Shrugged: 35th Anniversary Edition* (Signet, 1992), p. 937.

CHAPTER NINE

1. Ayn Rand's quote is from "Intellectual Ammunition Department" of April 1962 issue of *The Objectivist Newsletter*. The issue is collected in *The Objectivist Newsletter, Volumes 1–4, 1962–1965* (Second Renaissance Books, 1990).

2. See Ayn Rand's *We the Living: 60th Anniversary Edition* (Signet, 1996), p. xvii.

3. Ibid., p. xvii.

4. See Peikoff's *Objectivism: The Philosophy of Ayn Rand* (Meridian, 1993), p. 282.

5. The quote appears in Ayn Rand's *The Virtue of Selfishness* (Signet, 1964), p. 28.

6. See Ayn Rand's *Atlas Shrugged: 35th Anniversary Edition* (Signet, 1992), p. 940.

7. The quote appears in "Introduction to Objectivist Epistemology (V)" in the November 1966 issue of *The Objectivist*. The issue is collected in *The Objectivist: Volumes 5–10, 1966–1971* (Second Renaissance Books).

8. The quote appears on p. 51 of T. J. Rodgers, William Taylor, and Rick Foreman's *No Excuses Management* (Doubleday Currency, 1993). Chapter two details the Cypress appraisal system.

9. Ibid., p. 59.

10. A history of the exchange and the full text of T. J. Rodgers's letter are available at www.cypress.com.

11. A selection of Rand's letters to Hospers appears in *Letters of Ayn Rand* (Plume, 1997), edited by Michael Berliner. The quote is from a letter dated April 29, 1961, pp. 558–559.

12. See Ayn Rand's *Atlas Shrugged: 35th Anniversary Edition* (Signet, 1992), p. 937.

Chapter Ten

1. The quoted phrase appears in Ayn Rand's article "What is Capitalism?, Part 1" in the November 1965 issue of *The Objectivist Newsletter*. It is collected in *The Objectivist Newsletter, Volumes 1–4, 1962– 1965* (Second Renaissance Books).

2. See Mimi Reisel Gladstein's *The New Ayn Rand Companion, Revised and Expanded Edition* (Greenwood Press, 1999), p. 50.

3. The quote appears in Ayn Rand's *The Virtue of Selfishness* (Signet, 1964), p. 29.

4. See Ayn Rand's *Atlas Shrugged: 35th Anniversary Edition* (Signet, 1992), p. 387.

5. The quote appears on p. 292 of Leonard Peikoff's *Objectivism: The Philosophy of Ayn Rand* (Meridian, 1993). See pp. 292–303 for his discussion of productiveness.

6. Land's quote appears on p. 267 in *The Book of Entrepreneur's Wisdom* (Wiley, 1999), edited by Peter Krass.

7. The quote appears in Victor McElheny's biography of Land, *Insisting on the Impossible* (Perseus, 1998), p. 233.

8. The story of Sensormatic appears in Theodore Kinni and Al Ries's *Future Focus* (Capstone, 2000). The quoted phrase is on p. 312.

9. The quote appears in Victor McElheny's *Insisting on the Impossible* (Perseus, 1998), p. 163.

10. See Ayn Rand's *Atlas Shrugged: 35th Anniversary Edition* (Signet, 1992), p. 937.

CHAPTER ELEVEN

1. See Ayn Rand's *Atlas Shrugged: 35th Anniversary Edition* (Signet, 1992), p. 859.

2. The quote appears in Ayn Rand's *The Virtue of Selfishness* (Signet, 1964), p. 29.

3. *Atlas Shrugged: 35th Anniversary Edition* (Signet, 1992), p. 974.

4. The quote appears in *Introduction to Aristotle* (Modern Library College Editions, 1947), edited by Richard McKeon, p. 384.

5. *Atlas Shrugged: 35th Anniversary Edition* (Signet, 1992), p. 938.

6. Leonard Peikoff's analysis of pride appears in *Objectivism: The Philosophy of Ayn Rand* (Meridian, 1993), pp. 303–310.

7. Franklin's quote appears in Carl Van Doren's 1939 Pulitzer Prize–winning biography *Benjamin Franklin* (Penguin, 1991), p. 69.

8. *Atlas Shrugged: 35th Anniversary Edition* (Signet, 1992), p. 938.

Chapter Twelve

1. The quote appears in "The Money-Making Personality" by Ayn Rand in the April 1963 issue of *Cosmopolitan,* pp. 37–41.

2. The quote appears in "Progress or Sacrifice," by Ayn Rand, *Los Angeles Times,* July 1, 1962. All of the columns are collected in *The Ayn Rand Column* (Second Renaissance Books, 1998).

3. Edwin Land's quote, along with other aphorisms attributed to him, appears online at www.rowland.org.

4. The quotes appear on pp. 64 and 67 of George Gilder's *Wealth & Poverty* (ICS Press, 1993).

5. The quote appears in "What is Capitalism? Part II," by Ayn Rand in the December 1965 issue of *The Objectivist Newsletter.*

6. Ayn Rand's quote appears in the article "The Metaphysical Versus the Man-Made" in the March 12, 1973, issue of *The Ayn Rand Letter,* p. 2.

7. The quote appears in Roark's trial speech on p. 682 of *The Fountainhead: 50th Anniversary Edition* (Signet, 1993).

8. John Chamber's quote appears in "John Chambers: The Art of the Deal," by James Daly in the October 1999 issue of *Business 2.0.*

9. "The Money-Making Personality," *Cosmopolitan,* April 1963, pp. 37–41.

10. The quote appears in d'Anconia's Meaning of Money speech in *Atlas Shrugged: 35th Anniversary Edition* (Signet, 1992), p. 383.

11. The data on Glaxo Wellcome is drawn from *Future Focus* (Capstone, 2000), by Theodore Kinni and Al Ries, pp. 105–123.

12. Ibid., p. 387.

Chapter Thirteen

1. The quote appears in "The Objectivist Ethics," a speech first given at the University of Wisconsin, Feb. 9, 1961. It is reprinted in Ayn Rand's *The Virtue of Selfishness* (Signet, 1964), p. 34.

NOTES

2. Lou Gerstner's quote appears in Robert Slater's *Saving Big Blue* (McGraw-Hill, 1999), p. 67. It originally appeared in IBM's in-house magazine, *THINK*, No. 1, 1998.

3. Oticon's restructuring is described in Polly LaBarre's "The Dis-Organization of Oticon" in the July 18, 1994, issue of *Industry Week*, pp. 23–28.

4. The quote appears in Galt's radio speech in Ayn Rand's *Atlas Shrugged: 35th Anniversary Edition* (Signet, 1992), p. 940.

5. John Byrne's *Chainsaw* (HarperBusiness, 1999) gives a detailed account of Dunlap's hours-long harangue to the management team at Sunbeam on his first day as CEO.

6. Chalmer's statement appears in *Atlas Shrugged: 35th Anniversary Edition* (Signet, 1992), p. 559.

7. The fourteen points appear in chapter two of W. Edwards Deming's *Out of the Crisis* (MIT-CAES, 1986).

8. Gerstner's quote is on p. 216 of Robert Slater's *Saving Big Blue.*

9. The quote appears in Ayn Rand's "What is Capitalism? Part II," in the December 1965 issue of *The Objectivist Newsletter.*

10. Cypress's hiring procedures are described in chapter one of *No Excuses Management* (Doubleday, 1993), by T. J. Rodgers, William Taylor, and Rick Foreman.

11. Bill Gates's quote appears in Des Dearlove's *Business The Bill Gates Way* (Capstone, 1999), p. 62.

12. Ibid., p. 71.

13. *No Excuses Management,* p. 34.

CHAPTER FOURTEEN

1. The quote appears in Ayn Rand's "The Cashing-in: The Student 'Rebellion' Part III" in the September 1965 issue of *The Objectivist Newsletter.*

2. The quote appears in "The *Playboy* Interview: Ayn Rand ," by Alvin Toffler in *Playboy,* March 1964.

3. See Al Ries's *Focus* (HarperBusiness, 1997), p. xiii.

4. Craig Barrett's quote appears in "The New Intel," by Andy Reinhardt in the March 13, 2000, issue of *Business Week*, p. 110.

5. Ayn Rand's quote appears in Part II of her article "What Is Capitalism?" in the December 1965 issue of *The Objectivist Newsletter.*

6. See Howard Roark's courtroom speech in *The Fountainhead: 50th Anniversary Edition* (Signet, 1993), p. 678.

7. The quote appears in *Future Focus* (Capstone, 2000), by Theodore Kinni and Al Ries, p. 287.

8. Ayn Rand's quote appears in her article "Why I Like Stamp Collecting," in the Spring 1971 issue of *Minkus Stamp Journal,* pp. 2–5. It is reprinted in *The Ayn Rand Column* (Second Renaissance, 1998).

CONCLUSION

1. See "Followers of Ayn Rand Provide a Final Tribute," by Susan Chira, *The New York Times,* March 10, 1982.

2. Stanley Karnow describes Vietnam's economy since the war in *Vietnam: A History* (Penguin, 1997), pp. 41–49.

3. See "Putin's Advisor Extols Ayn Rand" by Catherine Belton, TheMoscowTimes.com, April 26, 2000.

4. Leonard Peikoff's quote is from his April 12, 1987, lecture at the Ford Hall Forum. It is reprinted in Ayn Rand's *The Voice of Reason: Essays in Objectivist Thought* (Meridian, 1990), pp. 334–353.

5. Ibid., p. 350–351.

6. Ibid., p. 352.

Index